Independence Bells
OF PHILADELPHIA

Independence Bells
OF PHILADELPHIA

THOMAS KAUFMANN

THE History PRESS

Published by The History Press
Charleston, SC
www.historypress.com

First published 2022

Manufactured in the United States

ISBN 9781467149587

Library of Congress Control Number: 2022943521

Notice: The information in this book is true and complete to the best of our knowledge. It is offered without guarantee on the part of the author or The History Press. The author and The History Press disclaim all liability in connection with the use of this book.

I dedicate this work to the honor and memory of my cousin.

Ross Thomas Hulslander
Corporal
A CO, 2nd BN, 503 Infantry, 173rd ABN BDE, USARV
Army of the United States

Born: November 21, 1947
Died: September 19, 1968

Died in action in Binh Din Province, South Vietnam.

And to all the men of his company, all Vietnam veterans, all armed forces veterans everywhere and in honor and memory of those who paid the ultimate price for our freedom and liberty. My deepest and heartfelt thanks go out to Sergeant Michael Picklesimer for telling me Tom's story forty-three years later, allowing the eight-year-old boy inside to weep at last.

And in memory of my late father, Andrew Joseph Kaufmann, and mother, Jane Lawson Kaufmann, from a grateful son.

Soli Deo honor et gloria.

CONTENTS

PREFACE

During my early years growing up in the late 1960s, I became familiar with the Liberty Bell and clearly remember an intriguing photograph of it in the *How Book of Cub Scouting*. It was and still is such an awesome and epic image of the bell, and it made a deep impression on me, making me interested to learn more about the bell, which looked to be so colossal to a young mind.

Around the same time, during my third- or fourth-grade year in school, I remember going to the bookshelf at the back of the classroom during the "quiet period" after lunch and finding a color-dyed, canvas-bound book about the Liberty Bell, with illustrations throughout—and I totally devoured it. Every page was such a fascination. Through this book, I became better acquainted with the story of the founding of our nation and the Liberty Bell, though I never gave much thought to the other bells in Philadelphia during the Revolution. This is because very little seems to have been written on the subject of Philadelphia's eighteenth-century bells—and the very little that has been written about them is not widely known. When I saw the Liberty Bell for the first time—after reading so much about it—the experience was simply beyond words. The opportunity I had to observe the bell for a short time was truly inspirational. It has a certain repose, but it also had the look of a battle warrior with many scars, and yet, it exudes victory, strength and hope for the future. Despite the crack (much of which was manmade), the bell appears to be in good form. No doubt, it's second and third casting left it with "character marks," and it is not as shiny and polished as it was in its

Above: Cub Scout and Scoutmaster looking at the Liberty Bell. *From* The How Book of Cub Scouting *(New York: Boy Scouts of America, 1951). Courtesy of Boy Scouts of America, Publishing Division, Irving, Texas.*

Opposite: The Liberty Bell in September 2020. *Photograph by the author.*

original form as cast by Lester and Pack (also known as the Whitechapel Bell Foundry, London). For all it has endured, it does not look any worse for the wear, yet absolutely embodies the spirit of America—that of a "rugged individualism."

What I did not consider—and was surprised to learn—was the fact that there were yet several more bells in Philadelphia, which have been tremendous contributors in the story of our nation gaining independence from Great Britain during the momentous events of 1776 and beyond. They played important roles in the historical narrative and were especially attractive items to the British as spoils of war to be melted down and recast as ammunition—or even cannon—or was it for a different reason altogether? In 1777 and 1778, these bells were especially at risk of being captured and suffering this fate. It may be said that they were at risk for a longer period of time, but truly, that is a discussion for another day. Interestingly, some years after the birth of our nation and the Revolutionary War, the Liberty Bell, then known as the State House Bell and later on as the Old State House Bell, grew in stature and honor and eventually became known as the Independence Bell—and finally, as its enduring and famous namesake as we know it today, because of its tremendous and central connection to the Declaration of Independence and American Revolution.

In like manner, all Revolution-era bells of Philadelphia indeed qualify for being known as *The Independence Bells of Philadelphia* because they, like the Independence Bell, very likely and most certainly rang on that glorious day in July 1776 and suffered with the "most celebrated bell" during the toils and strains of the Revolutionary War. Supposing for the sake of argument that if they did not ring then, they were, at the very least, silent witnesses to the birth of the "Great Experiment," as our nation is referred to from time to time. Some of these bells survive to this day, although some bells are gone, as well as their steeples. It is especially fitting now to tell their story, as America looks toward observing and celebrating the 250th anniversary of the signing of the Declaration of Independence on July 4, 2026—our nation's Sestercentennial. Very earnest research has been given to this work in order to find these artifacts in the records and verify them in their correct place—or as near to correct as possible—in the narrative of these impressive and historic old bells. This book also includes some of the untold stories of several other very important people who made Philadelphia and these United States of America so great. The reader will observe at many intervals throughout this book citations and excerpts from eighteenth-century records in which grammar may seem incorrect (including punctuations, spellings, et cetera). This was deliberate, as I tried to transcribe, as best as possible, the very essence of these handwritten notes into script so they could remain authentic at heart. This offers a unique glimpse into how our ancestors communicated, a fascinating study in and of itself. The original handwritten notes are so beautifully written. I hope you will enjoy and appreciate this intentional effect. I might add that it is so important to let the history speak for itself that even if the terms used by either the author or the historical sources cited seem offensive, no affront or disrespect is ever intended. We must let the historical record speak with complete honesty if we are to derive any benefit from it.

For the reader who is musically inclined and gifted, I offer my most sincere appreciation and congratulations to you for your gift and earnestly hope that you will know my deep appreciation for all things musical—which I've had for all my life. The sound of bells—whether chiming the Westminster and striking the hour, change ringing or played by the console of a chimestand or carillon—all affect me very deeply and always have. The musical aspect of the bells is the very center and essence of their creation and being. I believe that I would render a tremendous disservice to you, the musically gifted ones, if I ventured into commenting on the bells in a musical way without being a trained musician myself. But if what I have presented to you within these pages ignites and inspires you musically in knowing and understanding the wonderful company of these bells that have so blessed our great nation, then that will be reward enough.

Dear readers, it is my earnest hope that you will greatly enjoy reading about these very beautiful, excellent and wonderful *Independence Bells of Philadelphia*, which have contributed so much to the history of the city of Philadelphia and the founding of this, our great nation, the United States of America.

Thomas Kaufmann
Montgomery, Alabama
May 2022

ACKNOWLEDGEMENTS

Writing this book was like a dream come true, and I would like to so deeply and gratefully acknowledge those who made this work possible through their very kind and generous help. My deepest love and heartfelt thanks goes to my beautiful wife, Ann Marie, and our dear son, Tommy, who have been more than wonderful to me in their love and support of me in researching and writing this book. I also would like to express my heartfelt thanks to my dear family: Andy and Tina Kaufmann, David and Mary Grace Kaufmann, Kathryn Kaufmann, Russ and Jessica Coston, Joe and Katy Parson, Joe Kaufmann, Bryan Kaufmann, Mrs. Clyde Ashe, Victor and Ellen Hulslander, Brigadier General (Retired) Paul and Marie Majerick, Alex and Alane, Rowan and Wren Wyss.

I would like to express my deepest gratitude and thanks to:

- Karie Diethorn, chief curator, Independence Hall National Historic Park, National Park Service, Department of the Interior, Philadelphia, Pennsylvania.
- Robert L. Giannini III, former museum curator (retired), Independence Hall National Historic Park, Philadelphia, Pennsylvania.
- Alex Palma, assistant director, Carpenters' Company of Philadelphia, Carpenters' Hall, Philadelphia, Pennsylvania.
- Emily Smith, Digitization & Rights Coordinator, The Library Company of Philadelphia, Philadelphia, Pennsylvania.

- Andrew Williams, digital services archivist, Historical Society of Pennsylvania, Philadelphia, Pennsylvania.
- Edna J. Lemons, photo editor, Publishing Division, *Scout Life* magazine, Boy Scouts of America, Irving, Texas.
- Justine Kessler, digital services archivist, Historical Society of Pennsylvania, Philadelphia, Pennsylvania.
- Liberty Bell Museum, Zion's Reformed Church, Allentown, Pennsylvania:
    - Reverend Joshua Knappenberger, executive director and pastor.
    - Dr. Dennis Blankowitsch, president of the board.
    - Debbie Baldree, administrative assistant.
- John and Martha Eachus, Maryville, Tennessee.
- Bruce Butler (in memoriam), North American Guild of Change Ringers, Philadelphia, Pennsylvania.
- Christ Church, Philadelphia, Pennsylvania:
    - Reverend Timothy Browning Safford, rector.
    - Cecelia Wagner, church administrator.
    - Barbara Hogue, executive director, Christ Church Historic Preservation Trust.
    - Parker Kitterman, organist and music director.
- Jeanette Woehr, church historian, and Reverend Koshy Mathews, rector, Gloria Dei (Old Swedes) Church, Philadelphia, Pennsylvania.
- Mark Roberts, Gloria Dei (Old Swedes) Church.
- Michael Foight, director of distinctive collections and digital engagement, Falvey Memorial Library, Villanova University, Villanova Pennsylvania.
- Reverend Bill Waters, OSA, pastor, St. Augustine Roman Catholic Church, Philadelphia, Pennsylvania.
- Mark Galperin, campanologist and manager, Blagovest Bells, San Francisco.
- Konstantin Mishurovsky, keeper of the Spasskaya Tower Clock, Kremlin, Moscow, Russia.
- Camille Agricola Bowman, architectural conservator, Gadsden, Alabama.
- Andy Carroll, Scott Engineering Company, Opelika, Alabama.
- Professor Frank and Carol Walter, Opelika, Alabama.
- Kate Nelson, Opelika, Alabama.

- Nancy Donohue and Dr. Robert A. Schneider, archivists/historians of Old First United Church of Christ, Philadelphia, Pennsylvania.
- J.P. Meyer, archivist/historian, and Reverend Dr. Daniel Metzger, pastor, Old Zion Lutheran Church, Philadelphia, Pennsylvania.
- Juanita Roberts, executive director, library services, Tuskegee University.
- Reverend Chris Duncan, Trinity Presbyterian Church, Opelika, Alabama.
- Kevin and Terre Zackmann, Opelika, Alabama.
- Bill and Alisa Beck, Montgomery, Alabama.
- Gail Samuel, Ford Motor Company Library, Tuskegee University, Tuskegee, Alabama.
- Odessa Berry, Ford Motor Company Library, Tuskegee University, Tuskegee, Alabama.
- Professor Carlton and Brenda Nell, Opelika, Alabama.
- Jonathan and Melanie Underwood, Auburn, Alabama.
- June Pavelic Cutchins, Auburn, Alabama.
- Dr. Peter and Sally Ann Doyle, Auburn, Alabama.
- Ross & Tracy, Evan, John Merritt and Marshall Lee Leary, Montgomery, Alabama.
- Professor Rod Fluker, Robert R. Taylor School of Architecture and Construction Science, Tuskegee University, Tuskegee Alabama.
- Professor Jack Ames, Atlanta, Georgia.
- Tom and Kathy Watts, Opelika, Alabama.
- Dmitri and Olga Glotova, Auburn, Alabama.
- Charner Rodgers, PhD, Atlanta, Georgia.
- Frank and Robyn, Hannah, Royce, William and Amy Arnold, Opelika, Alabama.
- Ron and Marta Burgess, Opelika, Alabama.
- Dave Neel, Opelika, Alabama.
- Professor Norman and Mary Ann Godwin, Opelika, Alabama.
- Kevin and Kerry Dumas, Opelika, Alabama.
- Karren Pell, Montgomery, Alabama.
- Carole King, Montgomery, Alabama.
- Dr. Roger and Gail Lien, Opelika, Alabama.
- Tom and Diane Rickles, Opelika, Alabama.

- Veronica Cook, Auburn, Alabama.
- Reverend Bruce Bowers, associate pastor, Trinity Presbyterian Church, Opelika, Alabama.
- Jeanette Ligon, Tuskegee, Alabama.
- Karla Spratlan.
- Rod Wheeler, Tuskegee, Alabama.
- Allen Mendenhall, Auburn, Alabama.
- William Baker, Chicago, Illinois.

INTRODUCTION

This book is about an important part of American history—a history that has very likely never received the focus and attention it has deserved for the past 250 years—the story of Philadelphia's early historic bells. They are believed to have rung during the American Revolution—and there are several of them. Of course, the Liberty Bell has always been the greatest and most well-known bell among them, even worldwide. It's known as a symbol of independence, liberty and freedom, a proud emblem of and for America. However, it is rare—almost nonexistent, actually—that the average American would be so familiar with the following line from John Adams's letter to Samuel Chase on July 9, 1776, describing the events of the epic and eventful day before: "The Bells rung all Day, and almost all night. Even the Chimers, Chimed away."

Notice that Adams indicates not one bell but more than one—several, in fact. And it is not out of the question at all to surmise that practically "all of the bells in the City of Philadelphia-proper were rung all day, and almost all night—even the chimers, who chimed away"—if we take Adams's words as those coming from a man of character and integrity and not as hyperbole. This work is about those very bells; it seeks to confirm the historical accounts and traditional legends that declare that the bells did indeed ring on July 8, 1776, including the Liberty Bell. This book will endeavor to identify as many of these old Independence Bells of Philadelphia as possible, and in some cases, it will try to ascertain whether a few Philadelphia towers or steeples did, in fact, have a bell "in-situ" during the dawning of our new republic. This book will also explore how important bells were in everyday life—in striking the hour, opening assembly meetings, calling the faithful to worship, opening and closing the town market, ringing for weddings, sounding the alarm for fire and, sadly, tolling for the departed. As important as the historic bells themselves (and the historic tower clocks) are the people who built the towers and steeples, made the bells, created the clocks, rang the bells and kept the clocks running. Also of great interest is exploring how the early Philadelphians, with gritty determination, hewn out and built Philadelphia—from the heavy forest on the plain to a rustic village, which, in turn, became the beautiful red-bricked City of Brotherly Love. The city was situated between the Delaware and Schuylkill Rivers at the principal time and setting of our story, in which a number of buildings were erected on such meager resources that might remain unfinished for a season until funding was available for finishing the work—the Old State House (now known as Independence Hall) being a prime example, among others.

The accounts from this period are most compelling—in witnessing what construction was like in the seventeenth, eighteenth and nineteenth centuries, the difficulties and the triumphs—whether the task at hand was constructing a building, casting a bell, raising a tower, hanging or lowering a bell, finishing a steeple or even taking one down. In these accounts, we can see the very essence of the rugged American can-do spirit and individualism our nation is known for—but not apart from a great faith and trust in God for all things. It is the story of a great people who come from different walks of life, different races and creeds, yet united and inspired by the desire for liberty and freedom, both individually and as a sovereign, though imperfect, nation. Our nation required much forging and testing in the years following the Declaration of Independence in order to truly come ever closer to becoming the nation where liberty reigns supreme. This book's exploration into the *Independence Bells of Philadelphia* transports us through time to our present day, including a discussion about contemporary bells that are descendants of the bells of the Revolution and concluding with a look to the future as it relates to these historical and cultural treasures, emphasizing the need to continue the craft of making bells and tower clocks. It also points to the urgent need to conserve these highly significant artifacts of our American history and cultural memory for posterity and for the next 250 years and beyond as we continue to "form a more perfect Union, establish Justice, ensure domestic Tranquility, provide for the common defense, promote the general Welfare, and secure the Blessings of Liberty to ourselves and our Posterity."

1

SKETCHES OF BELLS IN EARLY PHILADELPHIA

Ordering Colonial Life in the City of Brotherly Love

Upon reading the early historical accounts of the Province of Pennsylvania, which is the principal interest of our story, it is quite natural to at once identify with its early beholders. It is a land that was originally inhabited by and acquired by a treaty with the Sachem Natives, a land bordered to the east by a bay-river suitable for harbor and to the west by a meandering river. In between, it was teeming with tall pines, hardwoods, oaks and all manner of wildlife. Soon after the arrival of William Penn in 1682, these natural resources began to give way to streets that were cut through the forest and thickets. Lots were cleared, houses and businesses were built and fish, fowl and wild animals fed the growing population of settlers in this new city called Philadelphia (from the Greek text in the Bible meaning the City of Brotherly Love). Over time, this new city took shape and formed in this pastoral setting as a most ideal community in which to live, recalling the prophetic exclamation "what a fine place for a town" from the passengers of the ship known as the *Shield* as it was plying the waters beside the site then known as Coaquanock (meaning grove of tall pines), in the year 1678, according to noted nineteenth-century Philadelphia historian John Fanning Watson's account.[1]

As the wilderness was cleared and structures were erected, one might ask when the first bell, or bells, appeared and were heard in this new town, beautifully situated between Delaware Bay and the Schuylkill River? At the time of this writing, the answer to this important question is not known. Hopefully, in time, the answer may be known. But we do know that at the

The British ship *Shield* plying the Delaware River, surveying the future site of Philadelphia. *Drawing by author, based on sketch from Watson's* Annals of Philadelphia.

time the settlement of the "Grove of Tall Pines" was founded, European bell foundries had been in "full bloom" for a very long time, casting bells for churches, town halls, places of industry and commerce and seagoing vessels of all types and kinds. In all probability, the very first appearance and sound of a bell in Coaquanock was from the first ship that arrived in Delaware Bay, and of course, this was multiplied by the increased number of ships coming to the harbor as Coaquanock became Philadelphia. Certainly, as buildings were erected and society was established, the need for bells was imminent and answered by way of ships transporting them from the European bellmakers to Philadelphia. And because of the English claims to the lands granted to William Penn, most of the early bells were very likely from British bell foundries. The earliest bells were most likely small to moderate castings in terms of size due to the limited strength of the late seventeenth-century wooden vernacular Philadelphia architecture. Later, as Philadelphia's population and revenues increased through growth in trade and the local economy, the city's architecture increased in size and mass due to larger occupancies requiring greater structural integrity—needed especially for belfries in order to hang larger bells, the larger size required for being heard over long distances, accomplished by placing the bell high in the tower—the tower bells of Philadelphia

Above: Early view of the Treaty Elm and the surrounding woodlands of the period. *Drawing by author, based on* Penn's Tree *by W. Birch, 1828.*

Right: William Penn. *Drawing by author.*

being this book's focus. The written references and accounts of bells in Philadelphia's early history are both varied and extremely interesting, ranging from the hearing of a church bell or bells to the ringing of a bell as a fire alarm—or to open and close the town market, strike the curfew or tell the hour, among other various purposes. Most certain were the contributions of many African Americans (sadly, as slaves) in the founding, development and growth of the new city, including the raising of towers and steeples and the hanging of bells, in all probability.

Of principal note: it is very likely that the earliest ecclesiastical bell in Philadelphia was the original bell of the Old Swedes Church, also known as the Gloria Dei Church, which was cast in Sweden in 1643, according to church records. The bell was in use at the first church building in Tinnicum (now Essington) until it was moved to the second church building in Philadelphia in 1700. The treatment of this very special bell will be discussed further and in more detail in a later chapter, but it was clearly one of the earliest bells in Philadelphia, a fact that is confirmed by other reputable sources. Among the many bells referenced in Philadelphia's history, the Old Market Bell seems to have had a more prominent place in the city's memory than perhaps other bells. John Fanning Watson, an eminent Philadelphia historian and author, wrote:

> *The 17th October, 1693—appears an order for the regulation of the Market by the governor and council, to be located in High street, where the Second street crosses it, and in no other place. That the market shall be opened twice a week by ringing of bell. That none shall vend, and none shall buy on the way, under a penalty. A clerk of the market is appointed, and his fees are derived from the sellers.*[2]

J. Thomas Scharf, a significant historian of Philadelphia and the author of *A History of Philadelphia, 1609–1884*, also describes this bell in his history of the city, including references to the 1707 Courthouse and the first market house:

> *On High Street, since called Market Street, there stood a mast supporting the great town bell. At the ringing of the bell, the people assembled to listen to the royal and provincial proclamations, city ordinances, etc., which were read aloud by the town-crier, or beadle, from a stand at the foot of the mast. In 1707 a court-house was erected on this site. It was a grand edifice for the time, and the early Philadelphians, who called it the "Great Towne-*

The Old Market Bell of Philadelphia. *Drawing by author.*

House," or the "Guild Hall," were very proud of it. Beside the assessments and fines devoted to that purpose, many worthy citizens contributed, by voluntary gifts of money, to the expense of its erection. The first permanent market-house was built in 1710, adjoining the court-house, from which it extended to about half-way to Third Street.[3]

Scharf's account provides a corroborative connection to the "great town bell" and its future location for historian Martin P. Snyder, writing almost a century later:

Opposite: A drawing of the Old Courthouse of Philadelphia (1837) by Philadelphia artist William L. Breton. *The Library Company of Philadelphia.*

Above: Drawing of the Old Courthouse being demolished on April 7, 1837, by Philadelphia artist William L. Breton. *The Library Company of Philadelphia.*

> *By 1698, a courthouse was projected for near this same intersection. It is marked for a plot to the west of Front Street, straddling the center of High Street. The second feature of the 1698 intersection was "the bell." This was the great town bell, erected upon a mast in the street, from the foot of which royal and provincial proclamations were announced. When the Courthouse was built, the bell was removed and installed in cupola of the low tower on the new building.*[4]

Thus, from these written records and other sources, we see that early Philadelphian life was very much ordered by the office of bells from their typically high stations throughout the city—although not all bells were hung very highly, such as Christ Church's very early 1702 bell, which was originally hung in the "fork of a tree" next to the church. We will learn more about this bell and its companion bell, cast in 1712, in the succeeding chapter. If we were able to observe early Philadelphia in the late seventeenth century and early eighteenth century, we would find that, indeed, there were a few bells that could be heard in the settlement, which later became the city, and there were certainly sounds of bells in the harbor. But ascertaining the exact number of bells in the city at that time does not seem possible; however, it is a near certainty that these bells were not large and ranged from being about a foot and a half in diameter and weighing about 80 pounds to being around two and a half feet in diameter and weighing 250 pounds. Larger bells required a significantly taller, sturdier structure along with the hardware necessary to enable a large bell to be mounted properly for swing-ringing by rope. Early Philadelphia's settlement architecture does not seem to have been that of a more permanent construction type; it was more on the order of "light framing," which could accommodate light bells. As we have gathered from the historical narratives, these early bells were not numerous but were an important part of Philadelphia's early life, bringing order, announcement, safety and a sense of well-being to citizens.

2

OLD ST. PETER'S EPISCOPAL CHURCH BELLS

A Gift of Two Bells

In 1753, the rector of Christ Church Reverend Dr. Richard Jenney met with a determined number of his parishioners who proposed that a new church be erected in southern Philadelphia. Jenney agreed to this at a later meeting with the church vestry, though his approval was granted somewhat reluctantly due to the thought of the consequences from such an initiative on his congregation. Yet in 1758, the church began moving toward the erection of a new house of worship and contracted with Scottish-born architect-builder Robert Smith, a member of the Carpenters' Company of Philadelphia, to build the new church. Frederick Lee Richards Jr., in his masterful 1992 thesis titled "Old St. Peter's Protestant Episcopal Church, Philadelphia, Pennsylvania: An Architectural History and Inventory (1758–1991)," raised a question concerning the authorship of design for Old St. Peter's: whether it originated and belonged to the vestry committee itself or was the product of Smith, who was highly esteemed as a master builder in Philadelphia. The design of Old St. Peter's bears an amazing resemblance to the Second Presbyterian Church, also built by Smith, in terms of plan, elevation and architectural detail. The most contrasting point of departure, architecturally speaking, between the two churches is observed in the type of belfry designed and built by Smith, as part of the original plan for Old St. Peter's was a wooden cupola, versus the extremely tall steeple of Second Presbyterian. The steeples of Second Presbyterian and Christ Church both dominated and defined the city's image exclusively during the middle of the eighteenth century because of their soaring height.

Above: St. Peter's Episcopal Church in 1829 by William L. Breton, lithographer-creator. *The Library Company of Philadelphia.*

Opposite: The first bells of St. Peter's, gifts from Christ Church to St. Peter's in 1760. *Drawing by author.*

According to Richards's excellent scholarly research, we have a very detailed description of the cupola itself, as it was proposed, and the extant remains of it that were found "under the roof" of the existing church:

> *That there shall be a Cupola Erected and Compleately finished on the West End of the said Building of Ten feet Diameter and at least Thirty-two feet high from the Top of the Roof to the Top of the Vane, that the said* [Robert] *Smith shall provide and fix thereon a large ball and vane composed of Copper and to be neatly Gilt* [St. Peter's building contract, August 5, 1758, CC Archives].[5]

And again, Richards tells us the historical narrative of how Christ Church donated two bells to St. Peter's Church for its new cupola:

> *On April 14, 1760, the vestry voted to donate "two old bells now in Christ Church" to St. Peter's for the cupola being constructed by Robert Smith. One bell was probably given to Christ Church between 1695–1702* [author's note: it was definitely given in 1702, per the casting

date on the bell], *while the other was acquired in 1712. The design of the cupola was rather generic, resembling many small cupolas on public buildings from the English Renaissance period. Its design source may well have been the plate in William Adam's Vitruvius Scoticus for the Orphan Hospital (1734–36) in Edinburgh. Adam's book actually contains views of several cupolas that resemble St. Peter's.*[6]

The Old St. Peter's cupola remained intact until it was dismantled in 1842 to make way for the present tall steeple designed by architect William Strickland and containing a peal of eight bells, all cast by Thomas Mears of the famed Whitechapel Bell Foundry in London, it's earlier bell founders, Thomas Lester and Thomas Pack, being the makers of Christ Church's bells and the bell of the Old State House, known in 1842 as Independence Hall, so named after the celebrated 1824 visit of the Revolutionary War hero the Marquis de Lafayette. Again, from Richard's research, there is more detail attesting to the presence of the cupola:

> *While the cupola is long gone, a number of significant features predating the 1842 bell tower do survive, providing clues to its construction and part of the church's original interior. The pulpit and reading desk are attached to a wall that forms one side of a brick tower that once supported the cupola. The top of that tower still stands within the attic above the church's main ceiling. A thick oak beam that once acted as one of three sill plates to carry the cupola's heavy weight remains, as do numerous other signs of the original framework. There is also a lower hidden space in the tower corresponding to the gallery level of the church. According to the original floor plan this was the "bell room," but more likely the bell ringers' room. The wooden flooring above this space (corresponding to the attic level) still contains two reinforced holes clearly designed for bell ropes. The "bell room" appears to have been whitewashed once, suggesting that it was a very bright space, especially since the middle window in the west wall at the gallery level opened onto it. That window opening, bricked shut since 1842, is clearly visible within the space. Other indicators within suggest that the present staircase to the pulpit and choir vesting room (second floor of the 1842 tower) was added in 1842, radically changing the spatial character within the old tower—note, for example, that the ground-level space behind the reading desk once contained the vestry room, according to the old floor plan.*[7]

What a fascination to learn that the archaeological remains of the base of the cupola are still intact and remain as a reminder of the story of the first belfry of Old St. Peter's, where its two bells joined others in the city in celebration, declaring independence from Great Britain on that memorable day of July 8, 1776. Equally as fascinating is knowing that even today, the 1702 Whitechapel Bell, indeed dated 1702 and not earlier, is extant at Christ Church in Philadelphia. And perhaps, one day, it may be rung on special occasions so that present ears might hear the same sound heard by founding fathers and others on that momentous day in July soon to be 250 years ago.

3

THE SECOND PRESBYTERIAN CHURCH BELL

"For Want of a Bell"

Greatly influenced by the revivalist preaching of the renowned eighteenth-century evangelist George Whitfield, a former associate of the founder of Methodism, John Wesley, the Second Presbyterian Church of Philadelphia was organized in 1743 as a "New Side" church, theologically speaking, versus the "Old Side" tradition of the First Presbyterian Church. To be clear, Old Side congregations practiced the faith of the Protestant Reformation in the tradition of the Reformation Fathers and were known to be more confessional, while New Side churches were more experimental in their evangelistic methods, et cetera.

In January 1749, the church was holding services at the Public Academy for the City of Philadelphia (a building believed to have had a bell in its cupola) until a new building was provided for the congregation. In parallel, the church leaders set about buying property and erecting a new building. In February 1749, the trustees of the Second Presbyterian Church bought a lot on the corner of Arch and Third Streets in Philadelphia that was suitable for building a new house of worship. Thereafter, they set down what would be the design and specifications for the new sanctuary in terms of size, types and placements of doors and windows, the type of roof and rafters and other building details. The trustees selected Robert Smith of the Carpenters' Company of Philadelphia (who was also the architect-builder of Old St. Peter's Episcopal Church) as the builder of Second Presbyterian Church. Given Smith's excellent reputation as an architect-builder, or master builder, if you will, the result of all of the labors to realize a beautiful edifice were

The Second Presbyterian Church of Philadelphia before its tall steeple was "carried up." *Drawing by author.*

not disappointing in the least, and on January 7, 1752, the first service in the new church was held. Many have commented on the similarities between the two buildings, although, in another sense, they are quite different altogether when more closely observed with more attention given to specific treatments and details. And of course, the single artifact that differentiated the two churches from one another was the yet-unbuilt steeple of Second Presbyterian, which would be practically as tall as the steeple of Christ Church upon its completion. Interestingly enough, an effort was made to begin the first phase of the steeple's construction, and on July 19, 1754, the committee met at the new church with builder-mason John Palmer, "who agreed to carry the Steeple up its full Height of Brick and Stone Work."[8]

The remaining future work on the steeple proceeded much more slowly based on the available funds for the steeple. In September 1755, a call was made for the amount of the steeple lottery account, and with no major activity commencing afterward, it was more than obvious that the funding was insufficient to do any further work. It was not until six years had passed, however, that movement resumed on the construction of the rest of the steeple:

A 1799 engraving of Arch Street and the Second Presbyterian Church of Philadelphia and its tall steeple by W. Birch and Son, Philadelphia. *The Library Company of Philadelphia.*

> *At a meeting of the Congregation on November 9, 1761, the parishioners met for the purpose of choosing a Committee for the Building of the Steeple, resulting in the following persons being chosen: Doctor John Redman, Nathaniel Magee, John Rhea, John Bayard, Gunning Bedford, Isaac Snowden, Jedidiah Snowden.*[9]

So, from the record we have, it appears that the steeple—the wooden portion of the bell tower—was completed by 1763. Renderings done by George Heap and, later, William Birch, do in fact show the Second Presbyterian steeple as being considerably tall, piercing the sky. The trustees were very concerned about paying off the debts accumulated by the steeple project and appeared to be doing everything in their power to retire the debt, judging from the trustees' minutes from November 1763:

> *At the meeting of the Congregation on Monday Evening November 6, 1763, Regular notice thereof being given the Sunday Preceding The Congregation being acquainted by the Manager for building the Steeple*

> *that they were in want of Money to pay off the Debts due on account of the Steeple, did agree that the hundred pounds now, now in the hands of Mr. Isaac Snowden should be paid into the hands of the Treasurer of the Committee of the Steeple.*[10]

After retiring the debt of the construction cost for erecting the steeple, it does seem like there was a cessation of work on the church and the steeple, generally speaking, for around six years—and no word is recorded as to the presence of a bell in the brick portion of the tower. However, Samuel Hazard had requested a bell as early as March 1749–50—and in very strong words written to his brother:

> *Bring us 2 or 3 good branches* [chandeliers] *& if you could add a very good bell to it we should like it the better, for you must know we intend to have a steeple and a handsome one, too.…In short if you don't get something handsome for us you must expect to be severely reproved when we see you if we proceed to no higher censure.*[11]

The reason for Hazard's threat of censure was very likely traceable to the rivalry between Christ Church and Second Presbyterian to have the highest, best and most beautiful steeple in Philadelphia. Several years later, in 1769, the desire for a church bell appears again in church records:

> *The Congregation have appointed Messrs. Bedford & Armitage to Collect in the Money formerly Subscribed for building the Steeple. February 9, 1769, The Committee taking into consideration the want of a Bell, desire Mr. Nevill Mr. Armitage & Mr. Harbison to take the dimensions & weight of the State House & Christs Church Bells & report to the next Committee.*[12]

It does seem as though Second Presbyterian had procured a bell early on and was intending to purchase another bell for the tower, so naturally, its members wanted to do their homework and come away with the appropriate size and weight of a bell for their purposes. That a team was sent to measure and determine the weights of bells is indicative of the church's serious intention and suggests, perhaps, of it inquiring after a Whitechapel bell, since the State House and Christ Church bells were Whitechapel castings. After this mention, however, the following records of the trustee meetings do not appear to contain a single reference—or, should we say, a clearly noted

The probable bells of Second Presbyterian Church, as they were likely hung in the brick tower and not in the wooden steeple that was "carried up" later on. *Drawing by author.*

reference—to a bell and very little pertaining to a steeple for the next thirty years. It is only in late November 1800 that we see any outstanding mention of the steeple:

> *November 12, 1800: Resolved, That the same Committee (of Repairs) to employ three suitable persons who shall make a thorough examination of the steeple in writing in the form of a report the situation thereof.*[13]

After the report was delivered to the Committee of Repairs, the committee took action in addressing some of the concerns presented by the workmen. The following quote is from the Trustees' Minutes a few months later:

> *April 18, 1801: The Committee of Repairs moved to repair roof on the north side of the church and that the upper part of the steeple be repaired without delay; & 2 of the workmen have given it as their opinion that the dome must be taken down in order to repair it—and at considerable cost, & there being a diversity of sentiment in the board on the subject, some supporting it will be more eligible to take down the Steeple than to repair it.*[14]

After taking action to remedy some of the ills facing the church edifice, the church leadership followed up in a meeting with the congregation on May 4, 1801, where it was decided to repair the steeple.[15] On June 24, 1801, the trustees met and directed that the steeple should be repaired and repainted if the Committee of Repairs deemed it necessary.[16]

However, the outcomes of the following trustee meetings were not what had originally been hoped—and the most damning news for the steeple came from the carpenter's report.

The carpenter's report from July 11, 1801, recommended that the entire wooden portion of the steeple be taken down.[17] At the July 13, 1801 congregational meeting, a vote was taken on whether to take down the steeple. The trustees also proposed that they devise a ways and means committee for rebuilding the steeple and that a roof be placed over the brickwork of the extant portion of the steeple.[18] On January 19, 1803, "The Committee Appointed to Take Down the Steeple report that the business is finished, and that the cost was $433.41."[19]

Sadly, the magnificent steeple of the Second Presbyterian Church was at last taken down, and though we see that there was foresight and vision to rebuild the steeple, it never happened. For the rest of its existence, Second

Presbyterian was relegated to having no steeple, and in time, it did seem that the extant brick base of the steeple was dismantled, leaving no trace of the steeple at all. All in all, it must be said that for a church to invest so much capital into building such a dramatic architectural feature of the church, which is specifically intended for the use of a bell, and never have a bell seems illogical. The planning, intention and funding references in the trustees' minutes seem to suggest that there was very likely a bell—or, even better, two bells. Unlike today, towers and steeples then were built for bells, as bells were the "voice" of the church to summon worshippers and were rung for other occasions and in other capacities for the community. That being established, it would have been highly unusual for such a grand steeple in eighteenth-century Philadelphia to not have bells within it, rendering service for divine worship and other purposes—especially being rung in celebration of the birth of a new, free and independent nation on such a momentous day in July.

"Taking down the Second Presbyterian steeple" circa 1802, due to it suffering very severe deterioration over time. *Drawing by author.*

4

THE BELL OF THE GLORIA DEI (OLD SWEDES) CHURCH

The 1643 Bell—the Oldest Church Bell in Philadelphia?

In order to understand the bell of the Gloria Dei Church, or the Old Swedes Church, it is necessary to first understand the history of the Swedish people who ventured to the new world aboard the ships *Kalmar Nyckel* and *Fogel Grip* from the port of Gottenberg in 1637, during the reign of Queen Christina. The *Kalmar Nyckel* and *Fogel Grip* landed at the site of present-day Wilmington, Delaware, in early 1638.[20] The Swedes acquired land from the Minquas Natives in this area and named the settlement New Sweden.[21] This Swedish settlement was also known as Christina, in honor of the queen, who began her reign in 1632, after her father's death.[22] Imagine, if you will, what great natural beauty was beheld by these new settlers and why the land and the river were so attractive to them as a people—what opportunities to make their livelihoods lay before them, which appeared to be trading in furs and tobacco, chiefly. According to Gloria Dei Church historian Jeanette Woehr, all of this occurred six years before William Penn was even born.[23]

A few years later, around 1642 or 1643, Lieutenant Colonel Johan Printz arrived in New Sweden as the new governor.[24] Immediately taking inventory of the area, Printz decided that the existing settlement was not in the best site and moved the colony upriver to Tinicum Island, the site of present-day Philadelphia's International Airport. In this new settlement, he erected a fort (Ny Gottenberg, or New Gothenberg), a mansion (Printz Hall) and the first church in the region, the Old Swedes Church. This church began as a mission to the Algonquin Natives and was built of wood

Frank H. Taylor's 1922 drawing of the Gloria Dei (Old Swedes) Church of Philadelphia. *The Library Company of Philadelphia.*

and dedicated in late 1646 by its first rector, Johannes Campanius, and rector Israel Fluviander of Christina.[25] Before this time, accounts differ on exactly when—very likely around 1643 or 1644—the ship *Fama* sailed from Sweden to New Sweden with the bell that was destined for the mission church that was chartered on Tinicum Island. The author's research, at the time of this writing, could not conclusively determine records or documentation that certifies the maker of the bell. It is suggested, however, that the bell was possibly cast by Medardus Gessus, or Gerot Meyer, at the Royal Foundry in Sweden during this time, as their names appear on other bells from this same era in Sweden and present-day Estonia and Latvia. It is also very possible that any of the several other brass foundries in Sweden, such as the Skultuna Foundry, for example, could have made the bell. Known and extant Swedish church bells cast by Gessus/Meyer are marked by decorative and fanciful banding/inscriptions and the distinct "German lip," a very sharp-angled profile of the bell at the bottom. It is not out of the question to consider that the bell might have even been a royal gift of Queen Christina, since the Swedes' first settlement in the new world was named in honor of her. Upon its arrival, the bell was believed to have been hung from a tree until a belfry could be carried up near the church.[26]

Over time, the Swedes moved north again, into the part of the land known as Wiccacoa—the Leni Lenape name given to the area, meaning "pleasant place," quite the appropriate name given that the Swedes were very earnest in seeking peaceable relations with their Native neighbors.[27] It was here in Wiccacoa that a blockhouse (or fort) was built by the Delaware River, which became a house of worship upon the exit of the Dutch invaders from the colony.[28] In 1677, worship services were conducted on this site by Reverend Jacob Fabritius, with many members of the congregation being ferried to church by riverboats. In 1697, Reverend Andreas Rudman, the new pastor of the church, which came to be known as the Gloria Dei Church, or "Old Swedes Church," arrived from Sweden, along with two other ministers, Eric Bjork and Jonas Auren, who were to be the new ministers for churches in Delaware and New Jersey, respectively. Reverend Rudman was instrumental in building a house of worship almost right away—the cornerstone of the new church was laid in 1698—and the construction of the church took practically two years, being officially dedicated on June 2, 1700.[29] The 1643 bell was carried from the site of the old church in Tinicum and used at the new church in Wiccacoa, now known as the Southwark area of Philadelphia, so named by Penn. Whether the tower or a simple bell cote was built at this time is not clear, and again, it does seem likely that the bell was hung from a tree, as was the custom in Sweden and in the new world during that time.[30] When the steeple was erected, the bell was hoisted up, pulled into the steeple, and hung on a timber frame, as we can surmise from a reading of the interior of the belfry.

The 1643 bell of Old Swedes, as hung from a tree for ringing during the earliest days of the church. *Drawing by author.*

The Gloria Dei Church is the oldest brick building in Philadelphia, the oldest church in Pennsylvania and the oldest continuous congregation in America.[31] So, it begs the question: Was the 1643 bell the oldest bell in Philadelphia at the time of our nation's founding? Also, on the question of the bell's involvement in the birth of our nation, according to Gloria Dei Church historian Jeanette Woehr, oral history says that the Gloria Dei Church bell was active in ringing in celebration of the

"Heaving the 1643 bell of Old Swedes into the steeple." *Drawing by author.*

The Gloria Dei Church bell today. It was recast in 1806 from the 1643 bell by Philadelphia bellmaker George Hedderly. *Photograph by Mark Roberts, Gloria Dei Church.*

reading of the Declaration of Independence on July 8, 1776, and was also among the bells that were relocated to Allentown before the British arrived and occupied the city in 1777. This seems very plausible. John Adams's inference that "the bells in the city rang" appears to apply to practically all the bells within the vicinity of the State House. In 1777, any bell remaining in the city would have immediately been confiscated by the British. At the same time, the bell was no doubt very endeared to the heart of the congregation, since it was cast in Sweden in 1643 and was, by then, well over 130 years old and a treasure. Also consider that the commanding officers who carried out the order to evacuate the city also gave instructions on what to take; no doubt, bells and metals were priority items to move away from Philadelphia in order to further hinder the enemy's efforts as much as possible. Like the State House bell, the bells of Christ Church, Old St. Peter's and others in Philadelphia during the founding of our nation, the bell of Old Swede's was, is and always will be a noble patriot of liberty and freedom, even as it still exists within the recast bell of 1806 by Philadelphia bellmaker George Hedderly, surviving to this day in the steeple of Gloria Dei, bearing the following inscription:

> *CAST FOR THE SWEDISH CHURCH in PHILADELPHIA STILED GLORIA DEI. G. HEDDERLY FECIT, 1806, PARTLY FROM THE OLD BELL DATED 1643: I TO THE CHURCH THE LIVING CALL, AND TO THE GRAVE DO SUMMONS ALL.*[32]

5

OLD ST. PAUL'S EPISCOPAL CHURCH BELL

Working at the Wheel • Mending the Bell

Anyone studying the history of churches in Philadelphia and coming across images of Second Presbyterian Church, Old St. Peter's Church and Old St. Paul's Church, especially from the period when all of their belfries have been removed, will be apt to remark at the similarity of the three churches in their architectural design and appearance. This is no coincidence and speaks to the influence—yet again—of Philadelphia's architect-builder Robert Smith, who was the builder of all three churches. Again, though they are similar, they are indeed quite different from each other. Each congregation desired such a Georgian-inspired edifice, and each were constrained to build according to their own budgets, respectively—even Second Presbyterian in "carrying up" its lofty steeple when it did, as opposed to Old St. Peter's and Old St. Paul's, which both could not afford to have such a high artifact piercing the sky at that time.

Old St. Paul's, essentially finding its origin in parishioners from Christ Church (as well as some Presbyterians and Lutherans), held its first worship service at the State House, under the leadership of Reverend William McClenachan, with some three thousand persons in attendance on June 22, 1760.[33] From that moment, the path toward realizing the purchase of a lot on Third Street below Walnut Street and the erection of a house of worship was an expedient one, with the congregation worshipping in the new sanctuary on the Sunday before Christmas Day 1761.[34] From the very first, the vestry of St. Paul's was surely observing the work going on nearby at Old St. Peter's and knew the building talents of the able and gifted Robert

St. Paul's Episcopal Church without its cupola in 1859. *Photographed by Frederick DeBourge Richards; The Library Company of Philadelphia.*

Smith, whom they retained to build their new house of worship. St. Peter's and St. Paul's (both now known with the prefix "Old"), being similar in appearance, also shared a common structural component—the raised tie-beam truss design—which author-historian Charles E. Peterson maintains was adapted from Frances Price's *The British Carpenter.*[35] Smith's adaption of the truss became his own sign and trademark of his work. At St. Peter's, the truss spanned sixty feet clear, allowing the ceiling of the sanctuary to be arched and finished in plaster. And at Old St. Paul's, the span of the truss was sixty-five feet across, allowing for the same detail of an arched, plaster-finished ceiling.[36] In writing about bells, it is so important to understand the architecture of the buildings in which they are hung, especially if they were not hung in a self-supporting tower or steeple on the front elevation of a church or, in the case of Old St. Peter's, within the church's enclosure, as revealed by the remains of the brick tower for the cupola. At St. Paul's, the use of "raised tie-beam trusses" in the hands of the master-builder Smith would more than satisfy the dead weight of a belfry with a swing-ringing bell, which has the properties of its own dead weight along with its dynamic forces when ringing.

In the early stages of researching Old St. Paul's Church, the author began coming across images of the church that were disheartening at first. It had a simple yet elegant design, well-proportioned and beautiful—but with no tower or steeple. However, upon being introduced to the vestry minutes of St. Paul's Episcopal Church (1762–74), the picture became clearer, upon further investigation, concerning the presence of a bell and tower for the church. As a help to the reader: since payment and disbursements are given in English currency, the symbols below are defined to help readers interpret the symbols when reading the vestry minutes here and elsewhere in this book:

£ stands for pound, sometimes written as "L": 30£ or 30L
s stands for shilling: 30s
d stands for pence: 30d

From the vestry minutes of Monday May 16, 1763, which began with speaking about Reverend George Whitfield's soon-expected arrival, we find the following entry:

> *Order'd that Sam. Kirke Sexton shall be allowed the Sum of Twenty Pounds for his yearly Salary, on and above the further Sum of One Shilling p Week for ringing the Bell & the usual allowance for Sweeping the Church Christimas Easter & Whitsun tide.*[37]

And on Monday, April 30, 1764, we find that Kirk resigned from serving as sexton, being succeeded by Matthias Keen:

> *Mr. Samuel Kirk have declin'd Serving its Sexton to This Church the Vestry have appointed Matthias Keen to the Office & have agreed to pay him at the rate of L20 p Ann. till the Congreg. Meet at which Time the A Sexton will be Regularly Appointed by them.*[38]

Several years later, the January 1769 vestry minutes describe paying sexton Matthias Keen for his services but also paying him 0£, 3s and 9d, for "working at the Bell." It also described paying a Daniel Evans 0£, 6s and 0d for a "Clapper."[39] This entry not only further confirms that St. Paul's had a bell, but it also suggests that it was in need of repair—possibly a new clapper because the old one was broken. We may never know. The vestry minutes from January 17, 1770, seem to suggest that the bell was either not repaired previously or fell into disrepair again, as a payment of 0£, 10s and 0d was provided to Daniel Evans for "Mending the Bell," a payment of 0£, 7s and 3d, was made to a man named Smith for "working at the wheel," and 1£, 4s and 0d, was paid for a "Rope."[40] It appears that after two attempts, the bell was repaired. From the vestry minutes of April 29, 1771, when the past year's accounts were reviewed, we find that the vestry paid 3£, 19s and 3d to "Negroes for Ringing the Bell from Christmas 1769 to Christmas 1770."[41] The bell ringer was shown as being paid in the records from August 19, 1772, which means the bell was working.[42] However, it fell into disrepair yet again, according to another account, which confirms more information about the bell. From the vestry minutes of April 12, 1773, the vestry paid either sexton James Harris or James Barnes 3£, 2s and 0d for "Ringing the Bell," while John Brandt received 1£, 0s and 0d for a "Bell Rope" and William Preston was paid 0£, 5s and 6d for "Mending the Bell Wheel."[43] These references explain a great deal more about Old St. Paul's bell (singular, not *bells*), especially the reference to a "Bell Rope," which cost an entire British pound, meaning it had to have been very substantial in thickness and in length. Also of interesting note is the mention of the "Bell Wheel," obviously, the wheel for the bell-rope, which turns the bell as it is pulled from below. This can only mean that it was mounted—not in a tree, the fork of a tree or even on another type of bell mount stand. It would not have made sense to have a bell mounted on a low pedestal and rung by a rope. The only logical explanation is that this bell was hung in a belfry mounted on the church roof.

Once again, as we look into the vestry minutes from the better part of a year earlier, we find an amazing correlation:

> *At a Meeting of the Trustees of St Pauls Church on Monday 31 Aug 1761, the following were present:*
>
> - *Trustees*
>   - *Andrew Bankson*
>   - *Plunket Fleeson*
>   - *Ephraim Bonham*
>   - *John Knowles*
>   - *Walter Goodman*
>   - *Jn Ord*
>
> *Order'd that Mr. Smith prepare a Bill of Scantting for to Erect a hansome Cupola to St Pauls Church to be carried on Early in the Spring.*[44]

Basically, the trustees (vestry) members were placing an order for Robert Smith to make a list of costs involved and to do so as the selected builder while still demonstrating how cost effectively it may be done—as if he was seeking to be the lowest bidder in a contest to win the award of a contract to build the cupola. The trustees wanted a nice (and obviously well-built) cupola, but naturally, they wanted it done as feasibly as possible. And they wanted it done by "Early in the Spring." Of interesting note, which seems to totally corroborate the charge given to Robert Smith in August 1761, is a schedule of fees for funeral services in the vestry minutes of April 19, 1762:

> *Ordered that the fees hereafter to be demanded & used for Funerals be as follows.*
> *To the Minister for attending a Funeral Six Shillings.*
> *To the Clerk for the same Service Four Shillings.*
> *To the Sexton for Ringing the Bell Two Shillings.*
> *To the same for Digging the Grave Four Shillings & Six pence.*
> *To the Church for Breaking the Ground Ten Shillings.*
> *To the Church for being Buried within the Walls of the House Ten Pounds.*[45]

Most convincingly, based on the aforementioned list of fees for funeral services, Robert Smith indeed built the desired "hansome" cupola of St. Paul's Episcopal Church as so ordered—and he did so on schedule. The listing of the "Sexton Ringing the Bell" as part of the funeral fees appears to be the first mention of a bell in operation at St. Paul's. It is unfortunate that we do not know who made the bell, but since Christ Church had a relationship with the Whitechapel Bell Foundry (Thomas Lester/Thomas

St. Paul's as it likely appeared with its cupola. *Drawing by author.*

Pack), it is very likely that the bell came from them. It was a sizeable bell based on the information we have about the rope. Also, the mention of the bell needing repairs—a new clapper, repairs to the rope wheel and a new rope—altogether suggest that the bell was in heavy use and was perhaps being rung improperly, sustaining damage due to its size and weight. Perhaps the cause of the damage was "over-ringing" the bell, which was a common problem that was addressed by Paul Revere and other bell founders later on, with instructions on how to ring a bell as part of warranty conditions.

"Mending the clapper" of St. Paul's bell. *Drawing by author.*

Between 1761 and the turn of the nineteenth century, there appears to be very little information in the vestry minutes of St. Paul's regarding the bell—other than the occasional mention of payment to the sexton and his duties regarding the bell. There appears to be no other reference to the cupola. However, in the *Outline of the History of Old St. Paul's Church*, by Stanley Norris Barrett, there is an interesting footnote on page 43 that follows the mention of Richard Neave being buried in St. Paul's churchyard in 1795. The footnote references the cost of funerals at that time, including the payment of 2s and 6d to the sexton for ringing the bell (which was afterward given to St. Peter's Church). Curious. Could this perhaps be a clue in the story of the bells at St. Peter's, as well as for the discontinuation of bell ringing at St. Paul's due to the eventual dismantling of the Robert Smith Cupola?

On another curious and final note, adding to the intrigue of the bell(s) and cupola of St. Paul's, well after the days of the Revolution, on September 29, 1807, British-born church vestryman and generous benefactor John Keble passed away at the age of sixty-three, leaving St. Paul's with his house and lot on Pearson Court for the aged widows of the church, along with an endowment of $1,000, which was to be distributed as he wrote in his will: $250 for repairs on his bequeathed house, $250 toward the purchase of an organ, $250 for the construction of a cupola and $250 for the purchase of bells (as recorded in the vestry minutes from September 8, 1808) for the church.[46]

The aforementioned will proves that the original cupola was, in fact, dismantled, along with the bell (curiously said to be given to St. Peter's), leaving St. Paul's without either—until the gifts and stipulations from the will of John Keble appeared in the early nineteenth century. The fact that the church had a bell during the Revolution strongly suggests that this bell, confirmed in the vestry pages of Old St. Paul's minutes, did ring with the other bells in the city on that monumental day in July 1776.

6

BUILDING THE PENNSYLVANIA STATE HOUSE

And Yet Without a Steeple, Clock or Bell

Since the landing of William Penn at New Castle, Delaware, on October 27, 1682, ready to govern even before his transatlantic journey, the readiness of a prepared "house" in which to assemble for administrational purposes was unfortunately lacking within the domain of the colony, requiring the use of a number of seemingly "suitable" tenements or public buildings as required during the early period of colonial governance and according to the traditional and legendary account of Penn making the Friendship Treaty with the Leni Lenape tribe of Native Americans under the large American Elm Tree in the heart of Philadelphia, known forever afterward as the "Treaty Tree," also popularly known as the "Treaty Elm."[47]

The first assembly met at Chester on December 4, 1682, in a small brick house that belonged to John Hart. Realizing the need to trim down the size of the provincial government early on, Penn's reduction of required government personnel proved timely and aided greatly in working within the practical limitations of space for governmental meetings.

- George Guest's house, also known as the Blue Anchor Tavern (for council meetings).
- Old Swedes Church (for the first meeting of the Assembly of Pennsylvania).
- Laetitia Cottage, or Penn's Cottage (for council meetings).
- Governor's Residence, or Friends Meeting House/Bank Meeting House (legislature).
- Richard Whitpain House.

William Penn's treaty with the Leni Lape under the Treaty Elm in 1681. *The Library Company of Philadelphia.*

- Carpenter Mansion, or Slate Roof House.
- Whitpain House, or Shippen House.
- Public School-House (Thomas Makin, headmaster).

It wasn't long before serious discussions ensued about the erection of a dedicated House of Representatives for the body politic of Pennsylvania.[48] The enabling legislation of such was passed on May 10, 1729, but practically three years passed before ground was broken, in the spring of 1732, for the new edifice, which was designed by the Speaker of the Assembly Mr. Andrew Hamilton.[49]

Though trained as a barrister, Hamilton was capable as a "gentleman architect," much like Thomas Jefferson. One can only theorize that his latent talent belied a very keen personal interest and was obviously enhanced through personal study—again, like Jefferson, but also like Mr. Hamilton's local Philadelphia counterpart, Dr. John Kearsley, known to be the architect of Christ Church, whose opinions were no doubt offered on the design work of Hamilton for the new State House and rejected, on the whole, it seems, in favor of Hamilton's design proposals.

It would be interesting, to say the least, if it could be proven that Hamilton had consulted Colin Campbell's *Vitruvius Brittanicus* or perhaps the work of

Left: Andrew Hamilton, the architect of the Pennsylvania State House. *From Etting's* An Account of the Old State House in Pennsylvania.

Below: The substantially completed Pennsylvania State House, circa 1749, without the wooden steeple. *Drawing by author.*

Inigo Jones when developing his architectural essay for the new Pennsylvania State House, which was occupied for use by the assembly in 1735, although it was not totally finished at that time. The building proper was "substantially finished" around 1741 and stood for several years afterward without being "completely finished"—and without the erection of its proposed "Steeple," a term that is capitalized in all written references in the Assembly notes, along with the term "Bell."

Very sadly, Andrew Hamilton would not live to see the steeple raised to prominence or hear the peal of the State House Bell from the tower, as he died in 1741, more than a decade before the State House was thoroughly completed, the steeple built and the forthcoming State House Bell hung.[50] Of interest, there are some historical hints about the existence of a small bell that William Penn brought with him from England. It was said to be mounted near the front door of the building proper and was thereby used to summon representatives to the State House when the Assembly sessions began, as the State House was without a steeple at the time. The design of Hamilton's bell tower, however, retained a power over the minds and hearts of the members of the Assembly, who would not rest until it was realized.

7

"CARRYING UP" THE STATE HOUSE STEEPLE

A Steeple, a Clock and Two Bells

Upon inhabiting the State House, while it was yet unfinished, the members of the Assembly declared that the building should be completed—and without delay. Yet, in 1745, only the Judicial and Assembly Rooms were finished and ready for use, while other parts of the State House were no closer to being finished, the actions toward that end being stymied, chiefly speaking, by what seemed to be slothfulness on the part of the laborers. This, no doubt, wore on the patience of the Superintendents of the State House. However, the building was eventually completed by the end of the decade for full occupancy and use, and full attention then turned to the task of constructing the steeple:

> *On the 27th of January, 1750, the Assembly ordered "That the Superintendents of the State House proceed as soon as conveniently they may to carry up a building on the south side of the said house to contain the stair-case, with a suitable place thereon for hanging a Bell."*[51]

The late eminent architect-scholar Charles E. Peterson, FAIA, in his exemplary book *Robert Smith: Architect, Builder, Patriot, 1722–1777*, points out the distinction made by eighteenth-century builders between towers and steeples—in that, the former is made of masonry, and the latter is made of wood.[52] From several writings and references from that time period, this is very much borne out, though in today's construction lexicon, these terms, along with many others related to vertical artifacts of buildings, are

"Carrying up" the first State House steeple; building up the "brick tower"; and constructing the "wooden steeple," circa 1751. *Drawing by author.*

very much conflated. Regarding the execution of the order to realize the belfry, the work on the steeple did not proceed quickly; indeed, even in the Superintendents' letter from November 1, 1751, making a request for a bell from the Provincial Agent Robert Charles of London, instruction was given to make the bell ready for the workmen (superintended by Edmund

"Carrying up" the "wooden steeple" of the State House, where, within the cupola, the State House Bell was to be hung in its timber frame. *Drawing by author.*

Wooleyd) to raise and hang while the construction scaffolding was still in place on the steeple. The Superintendents' letter itself is most interesting:

> *Respected Friend, Robert Charles, The Assembly having ordered us (the Superintendents of the State House) to procure a bell from England, to be purchased for their use, we take the liberty to apply ourselves to thee to get us a good bell, of about two thousand pounds weight, the cost of which we presume may amount to about one hundred pounds sterling, or, perhaps, with the charges, something more....*
>
> *We hope and rely on thy care and assistance in this affair, and that thou wilt procure and forward it by the first good opportunity, as our workmen in-form us it will be much less trouble to hang the bell before their scaffolds are struck from the building where we intend to place it, which will not be done till the end of next summer or beginning of the fall.*
>
> *Let the bell be cast by the best workmen, and examined carefully before it is shipped, with the following words well shaped in large letters round it, viz.:*
>
> *"By order of the Assembly of the Province of Pennsylvania, for the State House in the city of Philadelphia, 1752."*
>
> *And underneath, "Proclaim Liberty through all the land to all the inhabitants thereof.—Levit. xxv. 10."*
>
> *As we have experienced thy readiness to serve this province on all occasions, we desire it may be our excuse for this additional trouble from thy assured friends,*
>
> *Isaac Norris.*
> *Thomas Leech*
> *Edward Warner.*
>
> *Let the package for transportation be examined with particular care, and the full value insured there.*[53]

Charles went to work in London, seeking to fulfill the provincial government's request for a bell for the State House, and retained London bellmaker Thomas Lester to cast the two-ton bell. Right away, the bell foundrymen set about to cast the requested bell, and upon a successful casting and curing, it was inspected carefully and then made ready for its transatlantic voyage to Philadelphia. It was believed to have come via the ship *Hibernia*, captained by William Child, according to John C. Paige and David C. Kimball in *The Liberty Bell of Independence National Historic Park: A Special History Study*. When the bell arrived at port and was brought ashore, it was said to have been "received in good order." However, it is at this point that the narrative account of what happened next to the bell appears to assume different versions from historical sources through the years:

> *One version of the story states that the bell was brought ashore and mounted upon a set of framed timbers, so that the bell could be tested (officially) for its sound and tonal quality, and at the first strike of the clapper, the bell fractured, and all seemed lost....*[54]
>
> *Yet another version maintains that when the bell was brought ashore and tested, it resulted in it being broken in two....*[55]
>
> *There is also one other version of the story—in that when the bell was in transit from the vessel to the steeple, it met with an accident that rendered its ringing qualities so imperfect as to create universal dissatisfaction and disappointment.*[56]

So, what are we to make of these various narratives regarding the fate of the bell after it left the Lester and Pack Bell Foundry on Whitechapel Road in London? Perhaps the most plausible interpretation of the historical account is that the State House bell, the product of Thomas Lester, the principal foundryman in the story, deemed to be a quality casting in London, was shipped to Philadelphia, whereupon arriving in late August 1752, it was received in "good order"; however, after it was set up in the State House Yard (Independence Square) for testing (upon the heavy timbers), it indeed fractured, affecting the sound in a most undesirable way and creating a huge dilemma for the Superintendents of the State House and the Assembly about what to do concerning this crisis that occurred so quickly in the early life of the bell.

In the past, Whitechapel Bell Foundry agents maintained that the bell was damaged during its reportedly stormy Atlantic crossing or tested incorrectly upon arrival.[57] Upon the discovery of the defect, the first suggested course of action was to send the bell back to the Whitechapel Foundry for a replacement bell, Superintendent and Assembly Speaker Isaac Norris pondered the matter

The arrival of the State House bell in Philadelphia, being set up in the State House Yard; the bell fractured upon it's initial test. *Drawing by author.*

The new State House bell, cast by Pass and Stow in its foundry in the "Vats" area of Philadelphia. *Drawing by author.*

most earnestly, and in the end, thought it was best not to send the bell back to London, but rather, seek out a local artisan who might remake the bell again and for the better. According to author Wellesley Bradshaw, in his book *History and Legends of the Old Liberty Bell*, Isaac Norris was also versed in the mechanical arts, which would explain why he bore such responsibility for superintending the State House, making him the natural connection to find those with the ability and skill to undertake such an important task. And Norris, in point of fact, was acquainted with and did request the services of two men, Pass and Stow, who owned a foundry that was said to have been located "in the fields" near the "Vats" on Third Street, in the vicinity of the Old York Road.[58]

Pass and Stow, by reputation being resourceful men, accepted the request and did indeed successfully recast the Lester and Pack bell into a new State House bell by March 1753, which was found to be stronger than the original casting after several tests for strength and tonality of sound. Norris was very pleased, as evidenced by the following excerpt from his letter below:

> *Pass & Stow have made a good bell, which pleases me much, that we should first venture upon, and succeed in, the greatest bell, for aught I know, in English America—surpassing, too, the imported one which was too high and brittle—the weight is 2,083 pounds.*[59]

Perhaps this event was a "Morningstar of the Revolution" moment, when the colonists, tired of their dependence on the mother country, were highly motivated to show their independence from Great Britain in manufacturing, trade and commerce. From Bradshaw's historical research, we can clearly see that there was substance to such a line of thought, as evidenced in a letter written to a friend by Norris after Pass and Stow made their mark, in which he sets about at the very beginning of his experience with the bell, after it was brought ashore, explaining the saga of the bell up to the present moment on March 10, 1753:

> *In that letter I gave information that our bell was generally liked and approved of, but in a few days after my writing, I had the mortification to hear that it was cracked by a stroke of the clapper without any other violence, as it was hung up to try the sound; though this was not very agreeable to us, we concluded to send it back by Capt. Budden, but he could not take it back on board, upon which two ingenious workmen undertook to cast it here, and I am just now informed they have this day opened the mould and have got a good bell, which, I confess, pleases me very much, that we should venture upon and succeed in the greatest bell cast, for aught I know, in British America. The mould was finished in a very masterly manner, and the letters, I am told, are better than the old ones. When we broke up the old metal, our judges here generally agreed it was too high and brittle, and cast several little bells out of it to try the sound and strength, and fixed upon an ounce and a half of copper to one pound of the old bell, and in this proportion we now have it.*[60]

And yet, when the Pass and Stow bell was hung in the steeple of the State House in April 1753, the tone was deemed to be unsatisfactory, and it was taken down and recast yet again by the "foundry in the fields." Let us consult historian John Thomas Scharf's work *History of Philadelphia 1609–1884* to take note of events pertaining to the new State House bell after it was brought ashore:

> *April 14, 1753. A native of the Isle of Malta (____ Pass) and a son of Charles Stow were the persons who undertook to cast our bell; they made the mould in a masterly manner and run the metal well; but upon trial, it seems they have added too much copper in the present bell, which is now hung up in its place; but they were so teased with the witticisms of the town that they had a new mould in great forwardness before Mesnard's arrival, and will very soon be ready to make a second essay. The second bell was cast and hung; it did not give great satisfaction, but was suffered to stay. It was hung the first week of June 1753. The bill for "sundries" served at the bell-hanging included potatoes, beef, bacon, mustard and other condiments, cheese, punch, bread, and beer.*[61]

Author and historian Frank M. Etting provides substantial evidence that the aforementioned "bill for sundries" for the bell hanging was given in celebration of the April bell-hanging occasion, even though they had to take the bell down once again for recasting to obtain a better tonal quality to please Philadelphians. It was hung again in June that same year, as reported by the nearby *Maryland Gazette*:

> *The* Maryland Gazette *of Thursday, July 5, 1753, published at Annapolis, says: "Philadelphia, June 7th, 1753. Last week was raised and fixed in the State House steeple, the new great Bell, cast here by Pass and Stow, weighing 2080 lbs. with this motto, 'Proclaim Liberty throughout all the land, unto all the inhabitants thereof.'—Lev. xxv. 10."*[62]

Perhaps there was a second celebration—let us hope there was—and may ongoing scholarly review confirm such a conjecture. Interestingly, Pass and Stow were paid in September 1753—later rather than sooner, it would seem—earning £60, 13s and 5d.[63] After some time had passed, it appears that there was still a controversy about the recast bell (the second casting) by Pass and Stow and the quality of its sound, so the Lester and Pack Bell Foundry was ordered to send over another bell of a similar make. When the

Heaving the State House Bell into the cupola of the steeple. *Drawing by author.*

Hanging the State House bell in its heavy, independent timber frame in the cupola. *Drawing by author.*

bell arrived, Speaker Norris opined that the difference between the two bells was "not that great" and made the decision to keep the Pass and Stow bell as well as the newly ordered bell cast by Lester around 1754, making for a very interesting chronology of the State House bell made by Pass and Stow, in terms of its various incarnations:

August 1752: The State House bell made by Lester and Pack (Whitechapel) arrives in Philadelphia
March 1753: The State House bell is recast by Pass and Stow.
April 1753: Pass and Stow recast their first State House bell.
June 1753: Pass and Stow's second recast State House bell is hung in the steeple.
August 1754: The Assembly resolves to keep the Pass and Stow bell and the new Whitechapel bell, or "Second Bell."

While most of the attention of the construction activity at the State House during these years seemed to be focused on the erection of the steeple and the acquisition of a bell that was suitable for the needs of the Assembly and the people of Philadelphia, there was another request on the part of the Assembly that was as earnest as its desire for a bell—and would have a direct relationship to it—and that was the expressed need for a public clock. The clock was to be so prominent that all citizens and legislators could keep time by it, and it would be so intrinsic in its workings that it would strike the hour on the State House bell—or at least that was the original thought on March 11, 1752, when the governing body of the province resolved and so ordered the procurement of such a clock with a large dial to tell time most visibly and clearly to all.[64] In a sense, both projects were set in motion in a parallel manner, though the struggle and controversy with acquiring a new bell for the State House steeple became much more of the focus and concentration of energy at that time. Perhaps this is why Speaker Norris was more than determined to have this clock made in America, as he put forth in a letter sent to a friend on March 10, 1753:

> *We expect it will prove better than any they would send us from England, where, when once they had it put out of their hands, they have done with it; but here the workman would be made very uneasy if he did not exert his utmost skill, as we do not stint him in the price of his labor.*[65]

Above: A view of Independence Hall, showing the Thomas Stretch Clock on the west façade. *Photograph by author.*

Left: Enlarged view of the Thomas Stretch Clock, always understood and interpreted as a large grandfather clock. *Photograph by author.*

Opposite: State House bell clock-bell, also known as the Second Bell or the Stretch Clock-Bell. *Drawing by author.*

Being a man with a deep sensibility and appreciation for the mechanical arts, Isaac Norris, no doubt, was very keen on retaining Philadelphia clockmaker Thomas Stretch, the son of the remarkable Peter Stretch, clockmaker extraordinaire, to make such a clock for the State House.[66] The Stretch clock was not fitted to the brick tower or steeple but was mounted inside the attic of the State House, directly centered on the massing of the brick tower, with rods emanating from it in both directions through pipes to clock faces mounted on both ends of the building.[67] At the west elevation of the State House, the clock face was mounted in a very unique architectural creation, a facsimile of a tall case clock, or a grandfather clock, a grand feature of the State House that is still standing to this day.

The Second Bell from the Lester and Pack Bell Foundry, though rejected as a replacement for Pass and Stow's State House bell due to non-improvement in tonal quality, was accepted by the Assembly in August 1754 and became the Stretch clock's stationary clock bell, or hour-strike bell, and was installed on the roof of the State House, directly over the Stretch clock, in order to better synchronize it with the clock's hour-strike mechanism to have greater efficiency and accuracy in time keeping.[68] No doubt, the Stretch clock was weight driven, with the clock weights located in chutes at the tower's corners,

requiring regular winding every eight days. The heavy pendulum of this clock certainly had a sturdy catch box directly below it to catch it in the event that it ever became detached from the clock and fell, crashing through the ceiling below into the building's second-floor hallway.

In terms of being compensated, the way in which Thomas Stretch was paid for his services is a curiosity, and Etting's following account errs in naming Peter Stretch as the clockmaker:

> *~~Peter~~* [author's note: Thomas] *Stretch was paid in 1759, for making this clock, and for taking care thereof for six years, £494, 5s and 5½d.*[69]

So, was Stretch paid only after he made the clock in 1753 and spent the next six years taking care of it? Perhaps this was the agreed-upon arrangement. If only we knew the answers. Stretch died six years later, in 1765, succeeded by Edward Duffield, who assumed caretaking duties for the clock in January 1762.[70] Duffield was, in turn, succeeded by David Rittenhouse in March 1775, and he superintended the clock for the members of Congress in 1776, when our nation was born.[71] For practically seventy-five years this clock saw good service until it neared the end of its tenure at the State House and was criticized for not keeping good time at all. And if the reader will forbear, we shall learn more about this important clock later in our story.

8

THE BELLS OF CHRIST CHURCH

The Tallest Steeple, a Ring of Eight

Since 1754 and the days following in mid-eighteenth century Philadelphia—and into the early twentieth century—any visitor to Philadelphia would be struck by the sight of the beautiful, impressive and inspirational steeple of Christ Church from most any direction. At nearly two hundred feet high, for a half-century, it was the tallest tower structure in America, gracing a grand and beautiful church edifice next to the Delaware River in Old City, only a few blocks from Independence Hall, where our nation was born. Anyone who searches through the history of the birth of our nation will find that Christ Church, in very good part, with other city churches, contributed so much to the founding of America, itself earning the moniker the Nation's Church—and indeed it was. George Washington, John Adams, Benjamin Franklin, John Penn, Robert Morris, Betsy Ross, Benjamin Rush and Frances Hopkinson were among the most notable attendees of Christ Church, among other notables and members of the Continental Congresses.

Christ Church was founded in 1695 by the Church of England and, of course, later became the very church where the American Episcopal Church was born in the United States. A "Reverend Mr. Clayton" was the church's first minister in a house of worship that was referred to by Gabriel Thomas's publication in 1698, which states that "the Church of England built a very fine church in this city in the year 1695."[72] Of course, beauty is in the eye of the beholder, as the ancient maxim declares, but there seemed to be negative opinions of the original church's aesthetics and its lack of size. The impression from history is that the original church was built of wood. Of

Above: Christ Church, Philadelphia. *From* Boucher's *The Historic American Building Survey*.

Opposite: The bell in the "fork of a tree," as recounted in the early history of Christ Church. *Drawing by author.*

interesting note is the description of the church's first bell, cast in 1702, which was suspended in the fork of a tree for use in divine service.[73]

Such a method of bell ringing, though not uncommon at the time, was surely very influential on the minds of the church's parishioners and vestry members. It seems that the church built a wooden bell tower after the church proper was constructed and in use for a time, and the bell that hung in the fork of the tree was most certainly moved into the belfry. Another bell, cast in 1712, was acquired later on, and was sharing space in the belfry with the earlier bell of 1702. An old artilleryman from Philadelphia, Captain Loxley, is quoted from Watson's first volume of his *Annals of Philadelphia* regarding the presence of two bells in the church's first belfry: "Of 'Christ Church,' he said it had a wooden belfry in the rear of church, with but two bells—the same now at St. Peter's Church."[74]

In concert with Captain Loxley's observations are the records of Christ Church's vestry minutes, whereby these two bells were indeed donated to the new church (St. Peter's) in 1760:

> *At a meeting of Vestry held at Reverend Doctor Robert Jenney* [Jenny] [Jeney]*'s April 14, 1760:*
>
> *Present:*
> *Reverend Doctor Robert Jenney* [Jenny] [Jeney]
>
> *Church Wardens:*
> *Henry Harrison*
> *Alexander* [Alex] *Stedman*
>
> *Vestry Men:*
> *John Kearsly* [Kearsley] [Kersley] [Kersly] *Sr.*
> *Townsend White*
> *Joseph Redmond*

John Ross
Evan Morgan
Peter Turner
John Sayer [Seyer] [Sayre] [Sears]
Jacob Duché [Dushé] [Dushee] [Dushea]
Charles Stedman [Steadman]
William Pywell [Pyewell]
James Humphreys
Edward Duffield
William Bingham

> *Ordered that James Humphreys, Townsend White, and William Bingham be a committee to settle the accounts of the late Church Warden Mr. Evan Morgan and make report thereon to the board.*
>
> *Ordered that notice be given to the committee for building the new church, that they make report of their proceedings to their board at their next meeting.*
>
> *Ordered that Church Warden Harrison, Mr. Jacob Duché* [Dushé] [Dushee] [Dushea], *and Mr. William Pywell [Pyewell] be a committee to superintend the repairs of the church for the ensying year.*
>
> *Resolved that the two old bells now in Christ Church be removed to the new church for the use of the said church, and Mr. Morgan is desired to see them there.*[75]

At the end of their service at Old St. Peter's, there are differing historical accounts regarding where each bell went afterward: One account states that the 1712 bell was given to Christ Church Hospital (also known as the Kearsely House) in 1876, and the 1702 bell was loaned to St. Peter's Church of Uniontown, Pennsylvania, in Fayette County for a time, until it was recalled to Christ Church in 1877 for use in its new chapel on Pine Street. Another account states that the 1702 bell was loaned to Christ Church Hospital (the Kearsely House) and was given back to Christ Church. The 1702 bell is now safely at home at Christ Church, where plans for it to be displayed were recently considered; indeed, it is one of the oldest extant bells in the nation.

Returning to the story of the origins of Christ Church's campanology: in the early eighteenth century, at a meeting at the house of Enoch Story on June 11, 1717, the vestry resolved "that a form of subscription be prepared by the Church Wardens towards erecting a steeple for Christ Church in Philadelphia to be laid before the next Vestry."[76]

A little less than three years later, alarming news came to the Vestry members at a meeting held on May 30, 1720, concerning the condition of the existing wooden belfry:

> *The belfry appearing very insufficient and rotten and* [there being] *great danger of the Great Bell falling unless speedily repaired*[,] *the Church Wardens are desired to order the clerk not to ring or toll said bell till further orders*[,] *and John Read and John Harrison are desired to view the said belfry and make report of the condition thereof* [at] *the next meeting of the Vestry.*[77]

It is difficult to glean from the records whether the belfry was repaired; judging from the previous record, the intent was to remedy the defective condition and make the bell(s) safe for ringing again. The "bad report" about the existing belfry most surely had an effect on members of the vestry in reassessing their priorities, goals and objectives regarding a church tower and bells—from the August 11, 1720 vestry minutes:

> *The Board, taking into their consideration the many inconveniences the Church at this time labours under, more particularly the want of room to accommodate diverse new settlers and others well wishers to the Church, who are forced either to stay at home or frequent dissenting congregations for want of seats, it is their opinion (there being no other way to remedy the same) that a voluntary subscription of the Congregation for the enlargement of the Church, the building of a Tower, and the purchasing of a set of bells be forthwith handed about and that the same be offered not only to all gentlemen and strangers resorting hither but to gentlemen of any foreign place well disposed towards the completion of so good a work.*[78]

As it turns out, the vestry did indeed create an account for a future steeple and bells, but there was no significant movement on the project until years later, on April 15, 1727, when the first building initiative was taken:

> *Then it was moved that the present Church was too small to accommodate the Congregation, and after some consideration had* [word missing] *thereupon and the necessity of enlarging the same being urged, Resolved, that an addition or enlargement of 33 foot be added to the west end of our Church, and that a foundation be forthwith laid for the same, together with a foundation for a steeple or tower adjoining to the west end of the*

> *enlargement. Upon which Doctor Kearsley, out of a hearty desire to have the said work begun, undertakes to set men a-digging in order to lay the foundation, and will disburse money for the same until subscriptions be made and collected for this use. Ordered that Mssrs. Robert Asheton* [Assheton][,] *John Kearsley*[,] *Peter Evans and Charles Read be appointed a committee to draw up proper applications for subscriptions from the parishioners as also from strangers for raising money for the above uses, and that they prepare another application for that purpose to be signed by the Church Wardens and Vestry, to be sent to St. Stephens* [uncertain] *under the care of Mr. Alexander Woodroop* [Wooddrop], *who is willing to transmit and negotiate the same.*[79]

On May 2 of the same year, the vestry heard a report on the progress of the work of laying the foundations of the thirty-three-foot addition and the prospective steeple:

> *Doctor Kearsley reported to the Vestry that he had ordered the digging and laying a foundation for the addition to the Church and also for the steeple and that the workmen were now about the same. Resolved that Mssrs. John Kearsley, Thomas Tresse, Robert Ellis and Thomas Leech be appointed overseers or managers of the work now begun, and that they take care that the work be well done and the workmen paid, and that a suitable foundation be laid for a handsome steeple to be erected when money can be raised sufficient for the purpose.*[80]

The work of transforming Christ Church from a small wooden church to an ecclesiastical edifice of Georgian magnificence was carried out over the next several years and was completed in the mid-1740s. Through the years, the feeling among later historians has been that Dr. John Kearsley, who was heavily involved in the construction of the church as a member of the vestry, was the church's "defacto" architect. He does appear to have been very interested in the architecture of the church and had quite a presence in the affairs of building the church, almost from the very beginning. So, now the church sanctuary was realized; however, there was only the footing of the proposed tower in the early 1740s, awaiting to be carried up together with an installation of a beautiful ring of bells, an unfulfilled desire of the church since 1717. A cursory look through the vestry minutes after 1717, through the following decades, reveals how often discussions of financing and planning the future steeple occurred—very much a case of fits and starts—and to the credit

Excavating the thirty-three-foot foundation for the future tower of Christ Church in 1727. *Drawing by author.*

of the church leadership, they never gave up. The story of Christ Church and its quest for a beautiful sanctuary, including its steeple, is an inspiring story. And it came to pass. In May 1751, with a steeple design by architect-builder Robert Smith, work on the structure began, fiscally administered through a steeple account book, while continuing the efforts to raise funds for the ongoing work at hand. Between 1751 and 1753, workmen quarried nearby native stone, made bricks and hauled vast amounts of sand and lime onsite for bricklayers to begin laying the massive walls of the tower with the cut and flattened stone, a task that took a generous amount of time. The structure was also faced with a brick veneer, creating a tower of incredible strength, supporting itself and the ring of eight bells, which were forthcoming a little later on.

Surely, this spectacle caught the gaze of many onlookers in Philadelphia over the period of construction, just as the church experienced in building the sanctuary, prior to building the tower. By 1753, the steeple was emerging above the skyline of Philadelphia, together with the Steeple of the State House; Second Presbyterian—the other "tallest steeple"—was not yet underway.

Once the masonry tower was completed, the workmen began building the wooden steeple with a grand design, and Robert Smith oversaw the work from the steeple's base to the brilliant gold-leafed, mitre-shaped finial

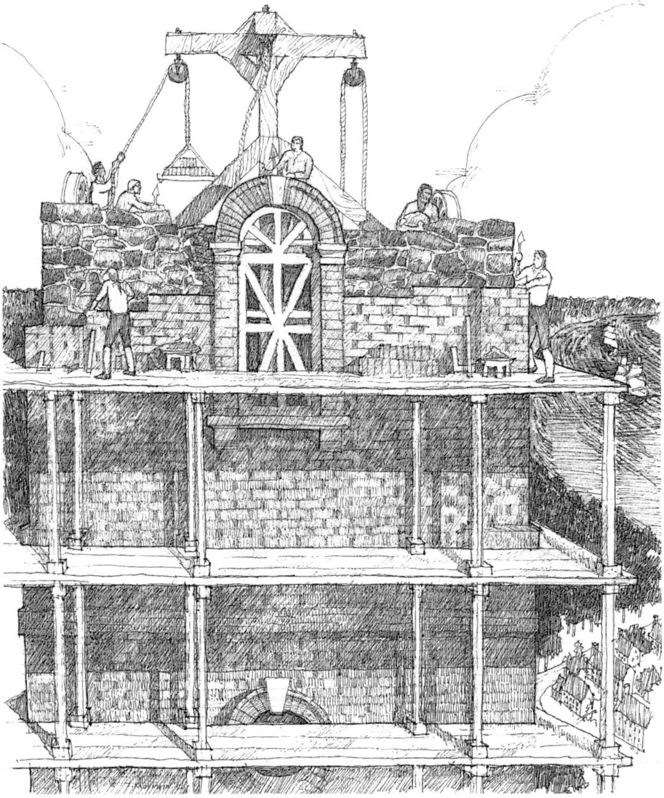

Left: Building the masonry tower of Christ Church from native stone and brick, circa 1751–53. *Drawing by author.*

Below: Philadelphia during the era of steeple building, circa 1754. *Drawing by author, based on George Heap's engraving from 1754; Historical Society of Pennsylvania.*

Opposite: The finial of the Christ Church steeple. *Drawing by author.*

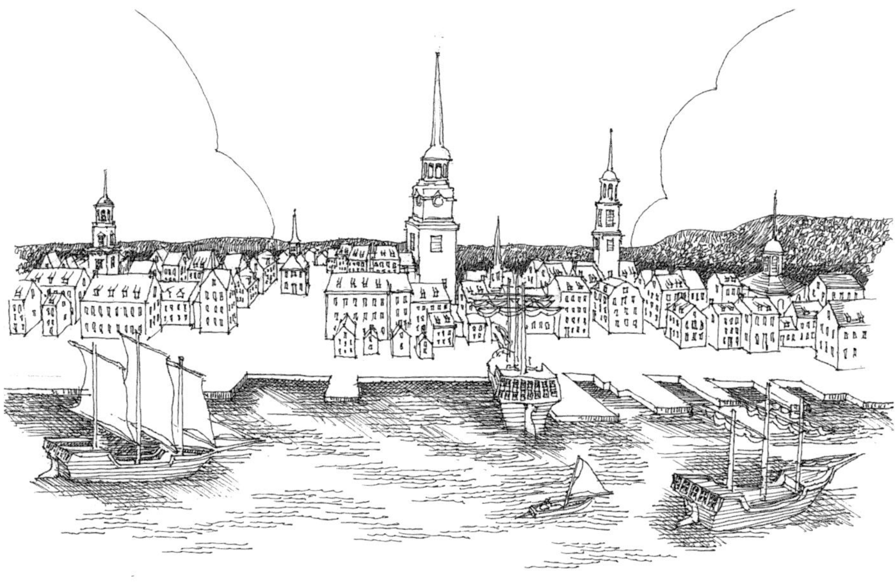

at the very top of the cupola's spire, a beautiful crowning element. The steeple was a magnificent gift for all Philadelphians to see—and beautiful it was and still is today.

As work on the steeple progressed toward completion, attention turned to the procurement of a ring of bells, as revealed through the vestry minutes of February 22, 1753:

It being represented to the Vestry that the sum raised by the sale of the lottery tickets; was not sufficient to finish the steeple; it was debated; whether a sum equal to that already raised; to be applied for finishing the steeple purchasing a ring of bells and a good clock might not be raised by a supplement to the lottery; and agreed to whereupon the following scheme was drawn up and ordered to be published.[81]

And several months later, on October 29, 1753, action was taken to obtain the bells:

The Vestry being met took into consideration what sum of money would be necessary to send to England for purchasing a ring of bells, and agreed that the sum of seven hundred and thirty-one pounds five shillings currency should be laid out in purchasing a bill of exchange of four hundred and fifty pounds sterling to be employed in purchasing a ring of eight bells, the tenor to weigh about eighteen hundredweight and the rest in proportion. And the treasurer is ordered to pay the said sum into the hand of Henry Harrison, who is desired to purchase the said bells. Townsend White, Peter Turner, and Henry Harrison are appointed a committee to remit the aforesaid bill and write to Mssrs. David Barclay & Sons and Mr. Lawrence Williams, merchants in London, to request their assistance in purchasing the aforesaid ring of the bells and send them to us on the easiest terms they can.[82]

Almost a year later, the vestry was settling accounts on the purchase of the bells with Barclay and Sons and Lawrence Williams, who had procured a ring of eight bells cast by the very same bell founders who had cast the State House Bell and the bell for the Stretch Clock, Thomas Lester and Thomas Pack, in their bell foundry on Whitechapel Road in London. For help in understanding "a ring of bells," the term refers to a number of bells that are cast together as a set for change ringing, a unique English tradition of bell ringing, the history of which, according to the North American Guild of Change Ringers (www.nagcr.org), originated as follows:

From the 12th century, the chiming of tower bells had been customary in all English villages to tell the time of day and to call people to church services. Ringing changes on these bells first arose around the year 1600 in the eastern counties of England, having been made possible by two parallel developments. The motivating development was the desire for the bells to be heard more broadly over the countryside and for the ringers to have more

Illustration of a ring of eight bells. *From Warner's* First Steps to Bell Ringing (London, 1881).

> *control over the timing of the sound. The enabling development was the replacement of the rope and lever, which had been used from the earliest days to sound the bells with, first, quarter wheels and then, by stages, the full-circle wheels that we still use today....*
>
> *The bells of the towers produce no recognizable tunes. Yet they are rung in sequences as disciplined and orderly as the stones and timbers of the towers themselves. These bells, rung in an ancient yet very modern way, produce a rich cascade of sound. This is change ringing. Change ringing requires special bells, special "music," and ordinary people who enjoy climbing towers, working as a team, and performing "The Exercise." The human ingredient is critical because change ringing is very different from playing a carillon or chime. It is not a single person sitting at a keyboard. There are no computers or electronic devices. Change ringing depends on real bells, each swung in a complete circle by a single person: six bells—six people, eight bells—eight people, usually standing in a circle.*

Another highly significant and interesting note about Christ Church's bells from the North American Guild of Change Ringers reads:

> *Christ Church's Bells are one of three rings of bells which were installed in the United States prior to the American Revolution. The Bells were cast by the foundry at Whitechapel, England, owned by Thomas Lester and Thomas Pack, the same firm which first cast the Liberty Bell two years before Christ Church's bells were cast in 1754. These are the only bells of the three original Pre-Revolution sets of change ringing bells which cannot be rung by change ringers. The Bells of Old North Church in Boston (installed 1744) were restored to change ringing in 1975 in time for the nations bicentennial and the Bells of Saint Michael's Church in Charlestown, SC, (installed 1764) were restored for change ringing in 1993.*

The bells of Christ Church were hung in late 1754 by Nicholas Nicholson, a native of Yorkshire, with an entry in the December 6 payment ledger of the steeple accounts book from the same year: "To Cash for Hanging The Bells—*£40.04*," along with entries from dates that followed for payments to others who were involved with the bells.[83] Of course, there was some ongoing work, it seems, on the wooden steeple involving Robert Smith, whose name appears in the steeple accounts book quite frequently between 1753 and 1754, receiving payments in part for his

Hoisting the ring of eight bells into Christ Church's steeple. *Drawing by author.*

Hanging the bells in the belfry of Christ Church. *Drawing by author.*

work of superintending the construction to conform to his design, which is traceable to the influence of William Adams and his steeple design for the Dundee Town House, circa the 1730s.[84]

It is at this point of the story of the bells of Christ Church that the author would like to provide a narrative describing the experience of climbing up to the belfry and seeing the bells firsthand:

> *Upon seeing the tower of Christ Church for the first time, its massiveness and height is daunting, imposing, aweing—and frightful. Frightful because of being informed of the "straight-up ladder" which one is required to ascend in order to see the bells. After years of exploring towers and experiencing many different types of ladders and methods of gaining access to belfries, clmbing up a straight-up ladder of tremendous height is still a challenge, especially when the ladder is original, well over one hundred years old, and located in the middle of the tower shaft. Even if the ladder is "new" and fabricated of steel, one wonders if the connections are solid at the top and bottom of such a ladder. One must be cautious and careful in any tower climb!*

Top, left: The Dundee Town House, circa 1735, by architect William Adams. *From Adams, Black and Robertson's* Vitruvius Scoticus.

Top, right: Christ Church steeple in September 2020. *Photograph by author.*

Bottom: The "winder stairs" in the steeple of Christ Church. *Photograph by author.*

The "metal stair" of Christ Church's steeple. *Photograph by author.*

The long "ladder stair" of Christ Church's steeple. *Photograph by author.*

To continue with the story of the tower ascension: entering the Christ Church steeple at the base, one ascends stairs in the tower's narthex to a small bridge over the entrance to the sanctuary, at the end of which is a door that opens to a quaint set of winding steps and stairs to the next level of the tower, where, upon reaching that stage of the structure, a relatively new steel stair leads to the last upper level before entering the belfry—so far, no straight-up ladders! In reaching the level below the belfry, which is a massive and vast void, one is immediately struck by the very long and angled ladder that begins near the west side of the tower and angles to the corner of the wall and ceiling at the east wall of the tower, where the access hatch is located. Suspended in the huge void while climbing the long angled-ladder, and reaching the access hatch, one encounters the surprisingly short, straight-up ladder, which is as tall as the depth of the floor supporting the belfry and the bells. At this point in the journey, adrenaline is racing, and suspense builds as you see the dim, shadowy stonework as you crawl up into the belfry, wondering where the bells are as you emerge from the hatch—and then, turning to your left—the bells silently welcome you into their domain!

The first sight of Christ Church's bells upon reaching the belfry of the steeple. *Photograph by author.*

An overhead view of the bells of Christ Church, circa 1935. *From* Historic American Buildings Survey.

> *It is a moment of awe, honor and respect when you realize what your eyes are beholding—the very bells that rang after the reading of the Declaration of Independence. They rang loudly all day and into the night, as history has told us. It is highly probable that, because the bells were being rung in change ringing fashion, they were heard above other Philadelphia bells, making a principal impression on John Adams as he wrote to Samuel Chase those incredible words: "The Bells rung all Day, and almost all night. Even the Chimers, Chimed away."*[85]

The magnificent heritage that belongs to the Liberty Bell belongs to these bells and all the bells that rang in Philadelphia on July 8, 1776. The bells of Christ Church appear to be mounted in their original heavy timber frame, along with what appears to be their original headstocks and hardware. And although some parts may be new, the general impression is that the bells retain their original appearance and character. The cast inscriptions, decorative patterns, reeds and other distinctive features still read clearly, and

A view of the massive timber bell frame where Christ Church's bells are hung in their wooden headstocks. *Photograph by author.*

Close-up view of one of the Christ Church bells. Inscription says "FECIT 1754" (made 1754). *Photograph by author.*

An enlarged detail of another Christ Church bell reveals "who" made the bells: Thomas Lester and Thomas (Pack). *Photograph by author.*

the bells retain their canons, the part of a bell that resembles a monarch's crown and straps the bell to the wooden headstock. This is quite amazing for bells that are, at the time of this writing, 268 years old. One unique feature of the tower construction for the bells and the bell frame is that the heavy timber bell frame was rotated diagonally, rather than installed foursquare, or at right angles with the tower's corners. This was done in a very solid framing plan of both simplicity and complexity. This method of assembly is rather ingenious, as it appears to concentrate the full impact of the bells' sound toward the belfry openings in each direction, and it also allows the bells to be more easily accessed for tuning and servicing. In the belfry, when gazing upward, one can see the handiwork of Robert Smith in the wooden structural base of the steeple above and marvel. Beholding such history, knowing that founding fathers ascended into this very belfry, that hands from the American Revolution touched these wonderful instruments and that ears from the Revolutionary era heard their beautiful sounds, one cannot help but feel so deeply moved.

9

THE GERMAN REFORMED AND LUTHERAN CHURCHES

An Empty Cupola, An Empty Tower, and Three Bells

The story of the German Reformed Church in Philadelphia begins with the migration of thousands of largely papal-persecuted, destitute, yet pious souls who came to the new world from Germany, Switzerland and even France in the early part of the eighteenth century, looking for freedom of religion, opportunity and a quiet and peaceful life in which they could work with their hands to earn their bread and earnestly enjoy the fruits of their labors. Many of the ancestors of the German Reformed Church in Philadelphia came from the Palatinate region of Germany under Reverend Michael Weiss, who organized the church and was its first pastor.[86] The early members of the German Reformed Church first worshipped in local residences and a butcher shop and then began worshipping in a small frame house around 1734. This house was shared with the Lutheran church (which will be discussed later) until the Lutherans began building their first brick church in 1743. According to tradition, the small house was, at first, said to have been a "barn."[87] And yet, better things were still to come for the congregation. In 1747, Reverend Michael Schlatter, the minister of the German Reformed Church, preached his first sermon in the new church, which, at the time, was without gallery or window and was unplastered.[88] This sanctuary was also the site of the first "coetus" or synod.[89] The church building was further described by Reverend David Van Horne in 1876:

> *This church building must have been of very quaint appearance, as shown in our cut. It was a stone or brick structure, hexagonal in form, with a hipped*

> *roof, sloping from each of the six sides to the cupola. The cupola was also hexagonal, with an arch-topped narrow window in each side. Surmounting this was a ball, pierced by a rod projecting to quite an elevation, with the figure of a cock (the usual Holland symbol), at the top, as a vane. In Scull and Heap's map of Philadelphia, 1753–54, the cupola is shown as that of the "Dutch Calvinistic Church."*[90]

Given that the church had invested in the construction of a cupola (and this was well documented), could there have been a desire for a bell to be hung in the cupola to announce the hour of divine service and serve in other capacities—as fire alarm and for weddings, funerals and other occasions? This author is of the mind that this was indeed the intent, especially given the German tradition of bells in the old country. Yet when we read the account of the first Sunday of worship in the building that was unfinished, it seems plausible that any procurement of a bell for the cupola would be impossible in the church's near future and very difficult even later on. According to Nancy Donohue, the archivist of Old First United Church of Christ, the descendent congregation of the early German Reformed Church, "the mention of a bell does not appear in the annals of church history."[91] However, members of the German Reformed Church did play a very important role in the American Revolution, as it has been said that they assisted with the removal of Philadelphia's bells from their towers for transport from Philadelphia to Allentown.[92] Still, the slight possibility exists that there may have been one, yet given that the second church building of 1772 had no steeple, tower or cupola, the probability of the existence of a bell seems very slim indeed. But the congregation still enjoys a special place in the rich tapestry of the story of the bells of the City of Brotherly Love.

In following the accounts from the German Lutherans in Philadelphia, especially after they left the small wooden frame house they shared with their German Reformed brethren around 1744 (John Fanning Watson says 1743)—and quoting from Watson again, he tells us that "the first church was built on Fifth street, at the corner of Appletree alley, and had a steeple affixed thereto, which had to be taken down in 1750, owing to having been erected too soon upon the new walls. This church was used by the British while in the city, as their garrison church, and the congregation using it also a part of each Sunday."[93] This church was known as St. Michael's Lutheran Church; in 1766, Zion Lutheran Church was built at the southeast corner of Cherry and Fourth Streets and became known in time as Old Zion Lutheran Church.

The German Reformed Church of Philadelphia, erected in 1747 and taken down in 1772. *Photograph by author.*

Above: The "New Lutheran Church" of Philadelphia, known as Old Zion Lutheran Church today, as engraved by W. Birch in 1800. *The Library Company of Philadelphia.*

Opposite: The German Lutheran School with what appears to be a wooden bell frame in the cupola. *The Library Company of Philadelphia.*

This fine old church was built by Philadelphia architect Robert Smith and possessed a highly decorated interior, which was gutted when the British occupied Philadelphia in 1777 and used Old Zion as a hospital. The building did have a steeple, which was as tall as the roof. And in this steeple, tragedy struck in 1794 when a wooden box of hot ashes was placed under its wooden stairs, and though they were thought to have been extinguished, they burst into flames, which spread throughout the church until the building was reduced to a brick shell of its former self. Despite the heavy burden of debt, the church was rebuilt between 1794 and 1796 with a proposed but likely never fully realized steeple, leaving one to conclude that during the Revolution, the Lutheran churches of St. Michael's and Old Zion did not have bells for their respective churches.

However, there were indeed bells that hung in the cupola of the German Lutheran School and Parish Hall at Fourth and Cherry Streets. Located just across the street from Old Zion, this building was used by the members

of Old Zion Lutheran Church as a meeting house and parish hall. It also gained historic notoriety for being the site of the first meeting of the German Society of Philadelphia.

Reportedly, there were three bells that were donated to the church for its use, yet the bells were hung in the cupola of the school.[94] In 1777,

Above: The bells of the German Lutheran School in its cupola. The German Reformed Church is visible in the background on the right. *Drawing by author.*

Opposite: The only surviving 1763 Bridgwater bell of the German Lutheran School, now at Old Zion Lutheran Church. *Photograph by J.P. Meyer, Old Zion Lutheran Church.*

church lore says that the largest bell of the three, along with the Liberty Bell and other city bells, was carried away from Philadelphia to safety. It's most certain that all three bells were carried away and returned together. The bells are said to have been returned to the schoolhouse and remained there until around 1870, when they were removed from the schoolhouse and given to the German Lutheran Cemetery near Thirty-First Street and Lehigh, and also around this time, a new church sanctuary was built at Franklin Square. The bells remained at the cemetery until the burial site was closed and reopened in a new location in 1960, whereupon the Old Zion congregation at Franklin Square received the largest of the three bells back again to the church, though the two smaller bells became uncounted for afterward. During the decade of the 1970s, the church building at Franklin Square was demolished, the bell being temporarily stored; meanwhile Old Zion merged with St. Matthews Lutheran Church, and the bell was again restored to the newly merged congregation, where it remains in the church's possession as one of its most treasured artifacts to this very day.[95] The bell, cast in 1763 by Thomas Bayley of the Bridgwater Founderies in Bridgwater, Somerset, England, is very rare, and is still rung by the church in announcing the hour of worship. The whereabouts of the other two bells remain unknown at the time of this writing, yet, perhaps, they may be discovered in the future in an obscure setting. Nonetheless, their contributions together in the birth of America will never be forgotten, and hopefully, will be recounted for generations to come!

10

CARPENTERS' HALL • PHILADELPHIA

The Signature "Robert Smith Cupola"

The Carpenters' Company of the City and County of Philadelphia was founded in 1724 and so chartered, in its own words, "to obtain instruction in the science of architecture and to assist such of its members as should by accident be in need of support, and of the widows and minor children of its members."[96]

James Portius was indeed one of the many highly significant and notable individuals who were members of this Company, whose contributions left Philadelphia with its early architectural legacy, including Independence Hall and Christ Church, among others. Portius came to the province with William Penn as Penn's exclusive architect-builder.[97] Portius amassed an incredible architectural library, which he left to the company after he died in 1736.[98] There is no doubt that the inheritance of Portius's library was central to the education of the prospective architect-builders of the Company, and was, in and of itself a chief resource, as Philadelphians called upon Company members to design and build their city. During this era in both American and architectural history—as it relates to the American Colonies—the profession of architecture had not yet developed and matured to the status of its counterpart in Europe, meaning that the American carpenter or mason was fully able to declare the title of "architect" in conjunction with his established trade title. It would not be until well over a century later that the profession of architecture would seek to define itself through education and licensing to distinguish itself from "every

Carpenters' Hall, as drawn by Philadelphia artist Frank H. Taylor in 1922. *The Library Company of Philadelphia.*

framer, carpenter and roofer" who declares the title of "architect"—although the fact remains that the earliest "architects" were builders as well as designers, even from the days of antiquity in Greece and Rome. Of interesting note is the interaction and subsequent conflict between the Company and the well-known British-American architect Benjamin Henry Latrobe, believed by many to be the nation's first professional architect. The conflict occurred when Latrobe established residence in the city, seeking to obtain important commissions—and was met with tremendous difficulty in both finding work and receiving the fees he desired. In his book *Benjamin Henry Latrobe,* the late and eminent architectural historian and scholar Talbot Hamlin summarized that the reason for the conflict between Latrobe and the Company was because of the well-established American architect-builder system (manifested by the company), which negated the need—and fees—for a European professional like Latrobe, who expected a fee of 5 percent of construction costs for his services.[99]

Carpenters' Hall was erected from the designs of architect-builder Robert Smith, complete with his favored vertical compositional element: the Cupola. Peterson holds the position that the building was designed by Smith but executed and built by other Company architects based on Smith's design.[100] From all that is known, construction began in 1770 and took the better part of the next three to four years to complete, all while being utilized for Company meetings and by other associations, including the Library Company of Philadelphia (started by Benjamin Franklin) and, ultimately, by the first Continental Congress, which was organized between January and July 1774, issuing their first list of the colonies' grievances to parliament and King George III in September 1774. Three years later, during the Revolutionary War, this entry appears from *Carpenters' Hall and Its Historic Memories 1876:*

> *When the British took possession, in 1777, of the city of Philadelphia, a portion of their army was quartered in the Hall, and continued there during the time they occupied the city. The soldiers made a target of the vane on the cupalo, and several holes were drilled through it by their bullets.*[101]

Carpenters' Hall has been, it seems, a much-sought-after site for convening meetings and even hosting tenants throughout its rich and storied history; in 1857, the Carpenters' Company discontinued the practice of renting spaces out to tenants and undertook a significant restoration of the hall, opening the building to the public for the sake of its significant history and role in the American Revolution.[102] The restoration attracted the attention and interest of the City of Philadelphia, which offered to purchase the hall, but the Company respectfully declined. Today, Carpenters' Hall remains the very same institution it always was, composed of architects, contractors and engineers.

Left: Carpenters' Hall today. *Photograph by author.*

Right: The interior of the Carpenters' Hall cupola. *Photograph by Alex Palma, Carpenters' Company of Philadelphia.*

With such an interesting and contributory history in the founding of our nation—and of the profession of the design, building and engineering arts—there is one question that remains about Carpenters' Hall: Did Smith's signature "Cupalo" ever have a bell hung within, ever? To answer, and after much inquiry and examination into the writings and sources available to the author at the time of this writing, the answer appears to be that it never had a bell, even from the beginning of its construction.

Why it did not have a bell is not known; it may have never been considered as a desired item, or the reason may have been because of the Companys' very stringent financial resources at the time of the building's construction. There is also no record of a bell ringing from the "Cupalo" of Carpenter's Hall on July 8, 1776, or of such a bell joining the company of other bells being taken down to join the seven-hundred-strong wagon caravan journey to safety in Allentown in 1777. And Carpenters' Hall was not alone in not having a bell; Independence Hall's flanking wings, Congress Hall and Old City Hall appear to have never had bells—only cupolas as "compositional elements" on their respective roofs. On many buildings—steeples, cupolas, domes and towers—are meant to be either purely architectural ornaments or attic ventilators. And for wonderful Georgian architecture, such as Carpenters' Hall, the edifice's cupola truly helps to define these beautiful buildings. The Hall was, is and always will be central and highly significant to our nation's history.

11

THE BELL OF THE WALNUT STREET GAOL

Keeping Order

In 1775, any Philadelphian walking along Walnut Street near the South Sixteenth Street intersection would not have missed the beautiful new building fronting Walnut Street—a grand edifice that would have been easily at home in London or another stately setting elsewhere in Great Britain. Made of beautifully hewn Pennsylvania stone, perfectly proportioned and crowned with a cupola on top of its central elevation in its "prendre parti," it would seem as though this design had come from the pages of either *Vitruvius Britannicus* or *Vitruvius Scoticus*—and most likely the latter—since the architect and builder of this magnificent example of Georgian architecture was believed to have been none other than Robert Smith, of the Carpenters' Company of Philadelphia. One might think that this structure was a grand civic building of some sort, or perhaps an academic institution or other type of building based on the fineness of its grandeur and sensibilities upon first initial glance, until they observed the pattern of the iron bars in each fenestration—opening of the façades where there should be windows—only. Even so, its aesthetic effect was such that it drew artists, such as James Peller Malcolm, to draw and paint it, even after they came to the realization that it was a *gaol* (the old medieval English spelling of "jail"). And for a gaol (or prison), it was one of the most beautiful of its kind. One would hope that beauty and good aesthetics would work toward reforming the occupants, and certainly, its attractiveness seemed to draw praise from Philadelphians as a civic contribution of the highest order. Peterson presents us with the conclusion that it could only have been Smith who built the prison, based on the scant information available to him at the time of his writing.[103] As

The Walnut Street Gaol, as depicted by W. Birch and Son in 1776. (Of note: other artists' renderings interpret an open cupola.) *The Library Company of Philadelphia.*

a further agreement with Peterson's conclusions, the building possesses the signature "Smith Cupola," which was indeed Smith's favored design for constructing belfries.[104]

It would be helpful for us to gain some insight, though unpleasant, into other descriptions of the prison. The following is a description of the prison written by John Fanning Watson in his *Annals of the History of Philadelphia*:

> *It stood on the south side of Walnut street opposite the State House Yard, occupying nearly half the block, and extending to the corner of Sixth street and running back to Prune street. It was built of stone, was two stories high, with a basement, and surmounted by a bell-tower. The centre portion projected a few feet, and was finished with a gable rising above the roof and breaking the long line of the cornice. The doorway was reached by a high flight of stone steps, which were flanked on either side by a one-storied structure, where were the offices or residences of the jailers' families. The northern portion—that is, the front on Walnut street—was occupied as the prison-house and prison-yard of criminals and convicts; and the southern, or Prune street portion, was used for the safe-keeping of persons*

imprisoned for debt or other civil delinquencies. Crime and poverty, then, were the tenants of the two apartments, separated by a courtyard, of the gloomy tenement which then occupied this place. Crime either languished in what was called solitary confinement, dark, idle, and uninstructed labor in a common and noisy workshop, the chief business of which was sawing stone—the most frequent, because the simplest of employments.[105]

From another chronicler of Philadelphia's history, we have South Carolinian Robert J. Turnbull's account of the Walnut Street Prison from his book *A Visit to the Philadelphia Prison*, written in 1798:

Premising thus much, and in further compliance with my promise of writing, I am necessarily induced to give you an account of the Philadelphia Prison. Notwithstanding a residence in this place for some months, I had never the curiosity till the last week, to visit this Wonder of the world. The expression is comprehensive but no less just; for, of all the Bridewells or Penitentiary Houses I ever read or heard of, I have met with none founded on similar principles, or which could in any manner boast of an administration so extensively useful and humane. Externally this prison presents itself as a very strong and secure building, constructed of stone, with a ground floor and two stories; and rather resembling an incomplete hollow parallelogram than any other form, with a north front on Walnut, and a south one on Prune Street. The principal front on Walnut Street measures one hundred and ninety feet in length, and forty feet in depth. The east and west sides or wings of the same depth, respectively, extend at right angles with the main front, ninety-five feet in a southern direction, and then join stone walls of twenty feet in height, running to the south-east and south-west corners. The west wing is on South Sixth Street. These three sides are appropriated for the confinement of criminals, vagrants, &c. and whose outward appearance does not much resemble a prison, but neat, handsome, and no inconsiderable ornament to the city.[106]

From Turnbull's observations, he confirms for us what we are most anxious to know—if there was indeed a bell in the prison's cupola—and what exactly was it used for in the daily life of the prison personnel and the prisoners (the following translation from the author):

At the approach of dusk the bell is rung, when they must leave off labor, immediately repair to their rooms, and form themselves in such a manner,

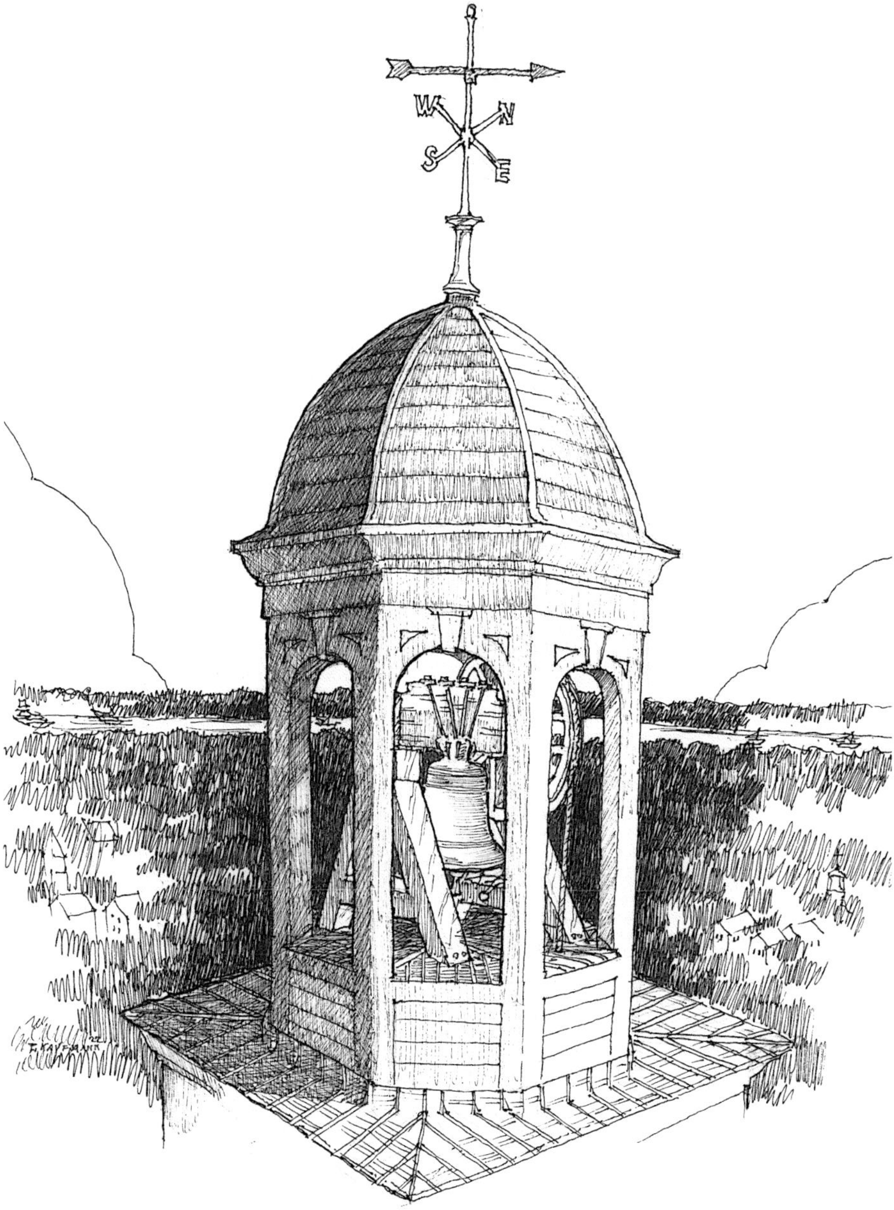

The cupola of the Walnut Street Gaol with its bell mounted within. *Drawing by author.*

> *that the keeper may have a perfect view of every person belonging to each room. They remain thus Formed, till he calls the roll, and counts them: he then locks them up in their apartments, but without candle or fire, except in extreme cold weather. From this time half an hour is allowed them to adjust their bedding, after which they are not permitted to converse aloud, or make a noise....*[107]
>
> *Four watchmen are obliged to continue in the prison all night: two are within the iron-grated door, and two in the inspector's room. In their turns they patrol the passages constantly, and strike the bell every hour. They report, on the morning of the succeeding day, any remarkable occurrence of the night, to the clerk of the prison, who commits the same to writing, and lays it before the inspectors at their next meeting...*[108]
>
> *The convicts are called to their meals by the ringing of a bell. We saw the Men sit down to their supper, and I do not recollect a scene more interesting.*[109]

From the aforementioned observations, it is clear how important the bell was in ordering the life and routine of the prison on a daily basis, especially as the prison did not have a clock, meaning that the bell was in fact, "the clock" of the prison.

If the reader will forbear with the author—although there is no further mention of any specific information given in regards to the bell from known available sources thus far, it is still possible to conjecture and make an educated guess about the bell and more details about it; since this prison was a large one, principally constructed of stone and brick throughout for reasons of security, it would stand to reason that a small to moderately sized bell would be an unlikely choice, as it would not be heard throughout the facility, whereas a large bell would be. As well, the bell of the Walnut Street Gaol would very likely have been mounted in a way as to accommodate being both a swing-ringing bell, and a bell that could also strike the hour. It appears that the bell was likely used in both ways, judging from the descriptions furnished by Turnbull. The bell was very likely employed through the method of swing ringing to call prisoners to meals and to retire from their labors at a day's end. And it was also very likely that it was struck while in a stationary position to announce each hour of the day and night through a device known as a striking or tolling hammer, which was typically mounted to strike the bell either inside its bowl or on its outside—above the lip of the bell. It was also possible to pull the clapper with a rope to strike the bell for telling time as well, although it would have been much easier to pull on a tolling rope below the bell on the hour, rather than climb into the cupola twenty-four times a day.

And yet, as to whether this bell rang together with the other Philadelphia bells on July 8, 1776—considered in the light of being freed from British tyranny in dual terms, namely, colonial rule and, with it, penitential rule—how could we so easily conclude that this colonial/penitential bell would remain silent during the time of such an epic and monumental turn of events in America?

12

JULY 8, 1776 • THE PROCLAMATION OF THE DECLARATION

"The Bells Rung All Day"

One basic belief that Americans know so well—and will tell you anytime, anywhere—is that on July 4, 1776, the State House bell (now known as the Liberty Bell) rang out after the signing of the Declaration of Independence. This belief is deeply embedded in the American psyche—and even the world over. And there are many so manifestations of the Liberty Bell in American culture, iconography, art and literature, where it is displayed, almost always, with a celebratory title and/or festoon banner with the well-known moniker of July 4, 1776. This is especially true around and on the Fourth of July holiday.

However, there is a belief that the State House bell (the Liberty Bell) did not ring on July 4, 1776, when the Declaration of Independence was signed—or at any time during the birth of our great nation. With the greatest respect to those who subscribe to this belief, the most earnest endeavor and inquiry was undertaken in seeking to find out what the pages of history had to say on the matter, and come to a conclusion. Most assuredly, nearly all—if not all—tower and steeple bells in Philadelphia rang on the momentous "day of celebration for the new republic," and we shall also endeavor to discover what happened with respect to those other bells that were rung, including the Stretch clock bell, which is often overlooked for being counted among the bells that rang out for Independence, probably because so little to nil has been written about them and their activity during the epic events of July 1776.

Above: The State House (Independence Hall) in 1776, as depicted by Louis Aubrun, lithographer, published by Thomas Hunter in 1876 for the Centennial. *The Library Company of Philadelphia.*

Opposite: The signing of the Declaration of Independence, July 4, 1776. *The Library Company of Philadelphia.*

In considering the Liberty Bell, before it achieved fame for the legend of "ringing on the Fourth of July," it was, as we have been told, known to all as the "State House bell" and had a central purpose in its office, which was to be rung to draw the Assembly into session, and the bell is mentioned as "ringing to summon," noted as such in the pages of the "Votes and Proceedings of the House of Representatives of the Province of Pennsylvania"—such as in the following notice from October 16, 1766:

> *Resolved, That such Members as do not appear at the Place of Meeting within Half an Hour after the Bell ceases to ring in the Fore and Afternoon, shall pay One Shilling; but if a Quorum be not present at the same time, then each Absent Member shall pay Two Shillings; and Eighteen-pence for every Hours Absence after, unless he can shew Cause to the Satisfaction of the House, which shall be determined by an immediate Vote.*
>
> *Resolved, that Mr. Richardson be, and is hereby appointed and empowered to collect and receive the Fines incurred as aforesaid, for the Benefit of the Pennsylvania Hospital.*[110]

So, we can see from the aforementioned "notice" how important the bell was in its principal office for calling members of the House into session

and how important punctuality was at the time. Many Representatives were surely mindful of the bell when it rang—after all, if they did not heed the bell's summons and were late for Assembly business, it would cost at least one shilling, if not more. Of course, the bell rang for other purposes, and at times, it rang so much that in 1772, the frequent ringing of the "great Bell" caused much consternation among local residents in the vicinity of the State House. On September 17, 1772, the House of Representatives, or the Assembly, if you will, considered a petition that was ultimately "Ordered to lie on the table for further consideration," which read as follows:

> *A Petition from divers Inhabitants of the City of Philadelphia, living near the State-House, was presented to the Chair and read, letting forth, that they are much incommoded, and distressed by the too frequent Ringing of the great Bell in the Steeple of the State-House, the Inconvenience of which has been often felt severely when some of the Petitioners Families have been afflicted with Sickness, which at Times, from its uncommon Size and unusual Sound, it is extremely dangerous and may prove fatal; that the Petitioners conceive that it was never designed to be rung on any other than public Occasions, such as the Times of Meetings of the Honorable Assembly of the Province, and of the Courts of Justice; that the Petitioners therefore entreat the House, to interpose and relieve them from this great and dangerous Inconvenience, so far as to prevent the Ringing of the said great Bell on any other than public Occasions.*[111]

From Peterson, we are told, that around the same time as the complaints/objections for ringing the bell, there were also concerns about the State House steeple's "insecure condition," and they were noted in the Assembly's minutes from early 1772.[112] Much discussion and deliberation ensued on the subject in January that year and at other times, such as the following—from the Minutes of October 19, 1774:

> *Upon Motion, The House took into Consideration the ruinous State-House Steeple, and after some Debate thereon, Ordered That the Superintendents of the State-house do take immediate Care to have the wooden Part of the Steeple taken-down, and the Brick Work cheaply covered to prevent it's being damaged by the Weather.*[113]

From the Minutes of the Assembly dated March 18, 1775, we learn that Robert Smith submitted a proposal to the House for removing the deteriorating steeple and tower down to the eaves and replacing it with a cupola—which was never realized.[114] Also, historian Frank M. Etting provides a very plausible account of the concern over the condition of the steeple from the mid-1770s to 1781, when it was finally taken down, from his book, *An Historical Account of the State House*:

> *Few alterations or repairs were made to the State House from the time of its completion to the termination of the Revolution. The steeple in which the Bell had been placed was of wood, and surmounted "the Tower" so-called. As early as 1771, Rev. Mr. Duche in his "Caspipina's Letters," tells us that the architecture of the steeple was considered so miserable that it was determined "to let it go to decay," in order to its better replacement. In 1773, a skillful carpenter was employed to view and report on its state; and the Assembly in the following year considered the expediency, and indeed gave the order, "that it should be taken down and the brick work cheaply covered to prevent its being damaged by weather." This order has given rise to the error of Mr. Watson, the annalist, and generally those who have since depicted the State House in 1776 have adopted his statement, inferring "what ought to be done, has been done"—but such was not the fact. Estimates were actually submitted in March 1775; it was then proposed to place a cupola upon the front building, but the subject was "referred for further consideration to the next sitting of the House." The Continental Congress met only a short time afterwards within its precincts; this circumstance, together with the pressure of the stirring events preceding*

> *the War of Independence, rendered further action impossible at the time. In April 1781, the condition of the steeple was considered absolutely dangerous, and was then, and not until then, pursuant to the peremptory order of the Assembly, taken down.*[115]

Given that there was a prevailing opinion about the steeple's terrible condition among the members of the Assembly, we must indeed still consider the following entry from Etting, regarding the bell ringing to bring the citizenry together to hear the most urgent news from the battlefield:

> *The Battle of Lexington and of Concord was fought on 19th April, 1775. The tidings reached Philadelphia on the afternoon of the 24th. Immediately notices were given for a public meeting, and upon the next day the State House Bell called together "eight thousand people by computation who assembled in the Yard," in order to consider what measures should be pursued. After several "eloquent and patriotic speeches," say the newspapers of 26th April, "the company unanimously agreed to associate for the purpose of defending with arms their lives, liberty, and property, against all attempts to deprive them of them."*[116]

Here, in 1775, we have highly contrasting events happening in the same year—a proposal made in March by Robert Smith to remove the deteriorated steeple and build a new cupola—and the ringing of the State House bell to call eight thousand people together to rally against the British. How contradictory! To complicate matters, in his book *The Liberty Bell* (1901), author Charles S. Keyser very compellingly presents a list of bell ringers for the State House bell, supporting the premise that the Assembly bell was never silent—from Keyser:

> *The Ringers of the Bell were Edward Kelly, 1753–55; David Edward, 1755–58; Andrew McNair, 1759–76 (September 15), the Ringer of the Proclamation of Independence. The last Ringer of the Bell was Thomas Downing, 1827–36.*[117]

Of especial interest is bell ringer Andrew McNair, who served from either 1759 to 1776 or 1758 to 1777, which was maintained by Mary D. Alexander in her book *Andrew McNair and the Liberty Bell 1776* (1929). He is more traditionally recognized as the "Ringer of the Proclamation of Independence," although, from Alexander, the historic annals of the Pine

Street Presbyterian Church of Philadelphia identify church member William Hurry as the man who rang the State House bell in July 1776. Interestingly, both men served as "Doorkeepers" in the House of Representatives. On October 15, 1771, McNair was also appointed "Doorkeeper to this House for the coming year." William Hurry also served as Doorkeeper when he was appointed to the post on March 4, 1777. The duties of Doorkeeper included being the bell ringer, among other duties, such as lighting candles in rooms, cleaning and occupying the Speaker's seat until the legislative session began. McNair served as Doorkeeper for the House in 1773, 1774, 1775 and 1776, until his death, which may have been in late 1776, in as much as we know.

However, the Minutes from January 11, 1774; October 19, 1774; and October 12, 1775, which entered the "Rules of the House for Regulating the Conduct and Attendance of Members," all curiously omit any reference to the ringing of the great bell:

> *Twenty-secondly, That such Members as do not appear at the Place of Meeting within Half an Hour after the Time appointed in the Fore- and Afternoon shall pay One Shilling; but if a Quorum be not present at the same Time, then each absent Member shall pay Two Shillings; and Eighteen-pence for every Hour's Absence after, unless he can shew Cause; to the Satisfaction of the House, which shall be determined by an immediate Vote.*[118]

Was the great bell not being rung as much due to the ruinous state of the steeple? As we have suggested before, this is curious. Was it possible that the bell was still performing its duties of office and simply not cited as such in the minutes of the Assembly? Further, Keyser's list of bell ringers supports the position that the bell did ring. It is here in our story that we should declare that, contrary to popular legend, the State House bell, our Liberty Bell, in all probability, may not have rung on July 4, 1776, as is commonly believed. Historically, through documented accounts from different sources, the overwhelming evidence for the date in which the bell was rung during the birth of our republic points to July 8, 1776, as the day when the bell rang with practically all the other bells in the city, after the reading of the Proclamation of the Declaration of Independence in the State House Yard by Colonel John Nixon. One of the best sources for verifying this premise is Wellesley Bradshaw's book *History and Legends of the Liberty Bell*—even though Bradshaw seems to confuse a "Captain Hopkins" with Colonel John Nixon as the person who read the Declaration to the large crowd that gathered in the Yard.

> *This bell was the first to ring out the Declaration of Independence on the eighth day of July 1776. We have conversed with many very old people about the facts, and their recollections of hearing in their youth persons who were then old, speak of the matter. There is much division about it. That the bell was not officially rung on the Fourth of July, seems to be certain. And there are some iconoclastic venerables who assert that it was not rung even on the eighth, which was the day on which the Declaration was first read to the people in the square by Captain Hopkins. But there can be no doubt that it was rung at that time, and it is more than likely that it was rung on July Fourth, though the other bells in the city were not.*[119]

The aforementioned narrative from Bradshaw deserves thoughtful pondering, in consideration together with the following account from Etting:

> *July 8, 1776, broke "a warm, sunshiny morning." The Committee of Inspection assembled at the Philosophical Hall at eleven o'clock, thence in procession proceeding to the Lodge, they were joined by the Committee of Safety; they then marched to the State House Yard and collected about the Observatory. The constituted authorities, including a number of the Delegates in Congress, filed out from the rear entrance to do honor to the occasion. John Nixon, a prominent member of the Committee of Safety, stood on the balcony or platform of the Observatory, the popular rostrum of the day, and, in a voice clear and distinct enough to be heard on the opposite side of Fifth Street, read aloud to the people, for the first time, the Declaration of Independence. The vast concourse of people greeted it by loud cheers and repeated huzzas. The royal insignia over the judges' seats were taken down and burnt, then the crowd left the square to exhibit, in other congenial ways in different parts of the city, their contempt for the King and his authority; assembling again at five o'clock in the afternoon on the common to listen to the proclamation to the troops and to join in bonfires, impromptu fire-works, and other demonstrations of joy. The night was star-light and beautiful. The old State House Bell made its Biblical quotation intelligible to every ear. For a quarter of a century its familiar tones had been the signal for assembling the liegemen of a foreign potentate; to-day it called together a sovereign people only to dismiss them with the benediction, all men are born free and independent.*[120]

And from Joseph L. Longshore and Benjamin Knowles's work titled *The Centennial Bell*, we have the following corroborative account of the bell from July 8, 1776:

> *It was at the instance of Mr. Norris, that this new bell was made to bear the beautiful motto: "Proclaim Liberty throughout all the land, to all the inhabitants thereof," which proved to be signally prophetic, for in less than a quarter of a century after, at the reading of the Declaration of Independence in the State House Yard, on Monday, July 8th, 1776, at 12 o'clock, to the populace, it proclaimed the glad tidings of the birth of a new nation, free and independent. From this day, it received the distinctive title of the "Liberty Bell," at the sound of which, the fires of liberty were kindled, and orators became eloquent. Its glory has been chanted in song, and its praises rehearsed in story until "Liberty Bell" have become household words in every family, and a theme of veneration on freedom's altar everywhere.*[121]

Although the State House bell achieved its greatest fame as the "Liberty Bell" several decades later during the abolitionist movement, it still must be deeply considered that it was so named because it represented the abolitionist cause as an emblem for furthering the realization of the constitutional rights promised to every American citizen. Given the premise of it being called the Liberty Bell at the beginning of the Republic would very well explain the description given "by another diarist of the times" (though not identified) in Alexander's scholarly work on Andrew McNair, which very much agrees with the accounts from July 8, 1776, of Frank Etting, Joseph L. Longshore and Benjamin Knowles, yet also takes note of the bell tolling (summoning the people together beforehand):

> *There was a large assembly in the yard who had been summoned by the tolling of the Liberty Bell as there had been many times before on the occasion of some public event. Passing through the assembled crowd the procession of officials, who had charge of proclaiming this state paper to the people, reached the platform, at which time the Liberty Bell ceased ringing. Colonel John Nixon, to whom the High Sheriff of Philadelphia had delegated the reading, stood up in the silence. He was a strong-voiced and open-featured man. He began reading with the words, "In Congress, on July 4th, 1776, a Declaration of the Representatives of the United States of America" and read through the important document, and it was accepted with general applause and beautiful satisfaction.*[122]

There are other accounts that attest to the State House bell ringing on July 8, 1776, along with many other bells. Probably the most oft-quoted historical record which supports this claim is found in a letter (the National Archives Foundation) that was written by John Adams to Samuel Chase on July 9, 1776:

To Samuel Chase
Philadelphia July 9, 1776
Dear sir,

Yours of the 5th came to me the 8th. You will see by this Post, that the River is past and the Bridge cutt away. The Declaration was yesterday published and proclaimed from that awfull Stage, in the State house Yard, by whom do you think? By the Committee of Safety! the Committee of Inspection, and a great Crowd of People. Three cheers rended the Welkin. The Battallions paraded on the common, and gave Us the Feu de Joy, notwithstanding the Scarcity of Powder. The Bells rung all Day, and almost all night. Even the Chimers, Chimed away. The Election for the City was carried on amidst all this Lurry, with the Utmost Decency, and order. Who are chosen I cant Say; but the List was Franklin, Writtenhouse, Owen Biddle, Cannon, Schlosser, Mattlack and Khull. Thus you See the Effect of Men of Fortune acting against the Sense of the People.

As soon as an American Seal is prepared, I conjecture the Declaration will be Subscribed by all the Members; which will give you the Opportunity you wish for, of transmitting your Name, among the Votaries of Independence.

I agree with you, that We never can again be happy, under a single Particle of British Power. Indeed this sentiment is very universal. The Arms, are taken down from every public place.

The army is at Crown point. We have sent up a great number of Shipwrights, to make a respectable Fleet upon the Lakes.

We have taken every Measure to defend New York. The Militia are marching this day, in a great Body from Pensilvania. That of Jersey has behaved well, turned out universally. That of Connecticutt, I was told, last night by Mr. Huntingdon, were coming in the full Number demanded of them, and must be there before now. We shall make it do, this year, and if We can Stop the Torrent, for this Campaign, it is as much as We deserve for our Weakness and sloth, in Politicks, the last. Next year We shall do better. New Governments will bring new Men into the Play, I perceive: Men of more Mettle.

> *Your Motion, last Fall for sending Embassadors to France, with conditional Instructions, was murdered, terminating in a Committee of secret Correspondence, which came to nothing.*
>
> *Thank you for the Paper and Resolves. You are attoning for all past Imperfections, by your Vigour, Spirit, and Unanimity.*
>
> *Send along your Militia for the flying Camp. Dont let them hesitate about their Harvest. They must defend the Field, before they can eat the Fruit. I shall inclose to you, Dr. Price. He is an independent, I think. My Compliments to Mr. Johnson, Mr. Carroll, and all your Friends whom I have the Honour to know, and believe me to be &c.*[123]

Adams was obviously an eyewitness and could only have been in central or near proximity to the State House Yard and the epic event that occurred before him. From Adams's letter, we know that the bells rang in the city on that momentous occasion. His assessment of the city bells ringing was a general impression, no doubt, which conveyed that most or nearly all of the bells in the city of Philadelphia were ringing, including the State House bell. If it was silent, given Adams's acute observation skills, would he not have noted it? Taken together with the other accounts, it seems very clear that the great bell did indeed ring on July 8. And yet, not all are satisfied with this conclusion, especially given that the greatest irony/contradiction appears to be the notion of "a ringing bell in a ruinous steeple." How can this be? We are at a deficit in having more historical information to know just how "ruinous" the steeple was at that time, especially in the way of more technical information, which would provide greater clarity and insight into the steeple's condition when ringing the State House bell.

At this point in our story, a hypothesis is offered by the author, based on his educational background and professional experience in architecture, historic preservation and observations of steeples and tower bells through the years, which will hopefully convince those who still remain skeptical about whether the State House bell did indeed ring, as we have learned, on July 8, 1776, after the proclamation of the Declaration of Independence:

> *The Old State House steeple was built by a good carpenter, Edmund Wooley, of great reputation with conventional four-square construction, and yet, was totally inexperienced with building any steeples at all (as noted by architect and author Charles Peterson).*[124] *Wooley's inexperience with steeple building very likely resulted in the omission of materials, methods and details necessary for proper waterproofing, especially during*

its construction. Consequently, the steeple sustained damage over several years to what was, in the beginning, very strong timber that was, no doubt, thoroughly inspected before use. According to architectural conservator Camille Agricola Bowman, the British tradition of building relied very heavily on the use of lead, a material of great longevity, for waterproofing. Perhaps Wooley's inexperience with the proper detailing for sealing the steeple was not as accomplished with the method the British employed in waterproofing their towers, steeples, domes and cupolas. Additionally, after the steeple was completed and in regular use, the structure was likely neglected for regular maintenance and repairs, which also contributed to the weakening of the steeple, most certainly because of the lack of available funds for maintenance due to the financial burdens and debts caused by the war. This type of passive behavior toward existing historic buildings is known in today's preservation language as "demolition by neglect" and has been a very common trait throughout the ages, in which the slow process of decay and ruin lead to the ultimate fate of a building's fragmentation and eventual and total collapse.

However, at the time of concerns about its condition, the steeple was obviously still self-supporting, and, in matters of observing a building or a building artifact for an honest appraisal of its structural integrity, a condition may, many times, appear worse than it actually is. Many times, conditions may appear "ruinous" when they in fact are not—or not to such a dangerous degree. Structural deterioration in buildings is, in many cases, a "slowly ticking clock." In many instances, water damage to a building takes years to develop to such a point that it causes structural collapse. Even though there were recommendations to take down the steeple, the fact that the steeple was still "holding itself up" is significant and obviously became a contributing reason for delaying its removal from the top of the original "brick tower," even though it was on track for becoming worse, and might not survive a tempest of severe weather, or may begin falling apart over time. On the part of the Assembly, the risk was obviously gambled on the belief that the steeple would not fall apart or fall down so soon, hence, avoiding the cost of disbursing funds for that purpose for as long as possible. Still, the major cause of anxiety about the condition of the steeple appeared to be the element of the unknown, beginning with the first observation of deterioration on the steeple and other similar observations that followed over the course of the next several years until it was taken down.

Further, the State House bell, from all accounts, does not appear to have been hung from the structural framing members of the steeple itself;

rather, historical references speak of the "bell and its frame" being a unit that was independent of the steeple's framing members—with the bell's frame being described as mounted upon/resting upon the steeple (cupola) floor. The bell was hung from its massive wooden yoke in this heavy timber frame. This description certainly fits with other accounts, such as Etting's, and speaks very plausibly to the issue of the continued use of the bell after the deterioration of the steeple was discovered, especially when we consider how the bell was, in fact, rung or intoned under such circumstances.

In this author's experience of observing bells in towers, it is not uncommon for a bell that was originally a swing-ringing bell, to become relegated to being rung by use of its tolling hammer, due to less than safe conditions for swinging the bell to make it ring. In fact, quite a number of bells in American towers today fit this description, rung by pulling on the rope to strike an unfortunately-stationary bell by the use of the tolling hammer. Architects and Engineers who understand archaic towers and steeples are best able to render a judgement pertaining to the level of structural integrity of a tower, and the effects of the dynamic forces of a ringing bell(s) acting upon it. The opinion of the campanologist is critical and essential in these matters and should be included in all discussions regarding towers, steeples and the bells (and clocks) within. At times, professional assessments may be surprising in that what may appear to be a concern for the towers, bells or both are, in fact, verifications of safe conditions for ringing. Stepping back in time to the decade of the statehouse steeple's woes, from the early 1770s to 1781, the members of the Carpenters' Company of Philadelphia were the equivalent of today's professional architect, builder or engineer in those days, and they could—and did—make assessments of various conditions in buildings all over Philadelphia, including the statehouse steeple, no doubt. We are not privy to all their conversations and discussions on the condition of the steeple, but very obviously, the steeple, although declared to be in need of being taken down, remained intact for several years with the State House bell, which is recorded as ringing at intervals before the steeple was removed. So, what does that tell us? It tells us that the steeple was deteriorating, though not so quickly. It tells us that the condition of the

Opposite: The Liberty Bell in its heavy frame. *From Etting's* An Account of the Old State House in Pennsylvania.

Above: Ringing the State House bell by its clapper on July 8, 1776. *Drawing by author.*

deterioration, in the beginning, appeared worse than it really was, but did begin to develop to a degree that was beyond the comfort level for allowing the steeple to remain in place. In all likelihood, during the evacuation of the State House bell to Allentown in September 1777, the required removal of water-proofing metals from the State House steeple would only be highly contributory to the acceleration of the deterioration of the wood framing, ultimately requiring its complete dismantlement in 1781.

For all of the aforementioned reasons, we may conclude that, at some point in the 1770s, the State House bell ceased to be rung conventionally on a regular basis by swing ringing, except on special occasions, and most certainly, it continued to be rung as it hung in a static position, either by pulling its clapper to strike the inside of the bell or by being struck with a mallet, as the steeple's condition worsened over time. Though this hypothesis is not empirical or even forensic in nature due to the absence of records of its actual physical conditions and context for scientific study—the steeple being long since demolished—it is hoped that the reader will consider this thesis in the light of the facts presented herein to support such a claim and conclude that on July 8, to be certain, the State House bell, indeed our Liberty Bell, did ring out with the other bells in the city in celebration of our nation declaring its independence as a free and sovereign nation from Great Britain and the tyrannical rule of King George III.

13

HIDDEN FROM THE BRITISH

Myth, Fact and Mystery

When word of the coming British invasion and occupation of Philadelphia reached the ears of the city's citizens, widespread panic erupted, as fearful citizens (Whigs, especially) began fleeing the city in order to reach safe destinations, leaving behind their homes, businesses and many of their possessions. Of course, Tories who were faithful to the British Crown remained, welcoming the troops into their city. However, as expected, the British did no small damage to the City of Brotherly Love. Several days before the arrival of the British troops, the Patriots began their exodus from the city, taking with them those articles they most cherished—both personal and public. How Providential it was that the Continental Army had the foresight to remove many, if not all, of the city's prominent bells from their towers and provide a way of escape for them to a place of safety.[125] Of course, the principal concern was over those bells falling into British hands and suffering the fate of being melted down and turned into either cannon/cannon balls or musket balls to be used on the already much beleaguered Continental Army.[126] At the same time, was there any thought about how important it was to save these bells out of respect and veneration for them, especially as iconic clarions for the Declaration and American Revolution? It is very difficult to conceive of this not being the case. The story of these bells' removal from their steeples and being loaded on wagons for transport to a haven of refuge is most interesting and remains the subject of academic intrigue and scholarship, even with respect to the established historical narrative that is familiar to anyone who has read about the history of the Liberty Bell specifically, which is that the bell was

Zion's Reformed Church, as it appeared in 1777. *Drawing by author.*

taken to Allentown, Pennsylvania, and hidden under the floorboards of Zion's Reformed Church in that city, along with the other bells that made the journey. Would it surprise the reader to know that there is another story about the Liberty Bell being taken to safety during those fateful days in 1777? There certainly was such a story. And because it was taken seriously for a time, it bears mentioning (author's paraphrase follows):

> *The story goes that in 1777, a small band of men, led by a Captain Thompson, went into the tower at Independence Hall and lowered the bell, under cover of darkness and a winter storm, onto a wagon pulled by oxen, and traveled in an easterly direction and sunk the bell in the Delaware River. This was supposedly the Liberty Bell's first dangerous journey away from Independence Hall since it was hung in the steeple. And since Captain Thompson was a prominent member at Christ Church, he was said to have convinced the vestry to take the same action with their peal of eight bells, which they did, sinking those bells into the Delaware River, near Trenton, New Jersey. Then, at the end of the war, when it was safe, the bells were restored to their places of prominence in the belfries of the State House and Christ Church, respectively.*[127]

Though the preceding story seems believable, the veracity of it has never been borne out. And yet, there was another element at work in the circulation of this account and others like it, pertaining to the routes and destinations of these bells, in that these stories are believed to be examples of "disinformation"—directed and promulgated by none other than General George Washington himself—who was known as a "spymaster," according to Reverend J.D. Knappenberger, the author of the outstanding historical narrative *The Liberty Bell at Zion's Reformed Church: How the Hiding of a Bell Impacted the World*. Reverend Knappenberger's premise regarding Washington's mastery of spying is more than confirmed by author David Hackett Fischer's *Washington's Crossing* and author Alexander Rose's *Washington's Spies*. In his narrative, Reverend Knappenberger, the Director of the Liberty Bell Museum, presents very compelling reasons for why the mission of transporting bells and metals out of Philadelphia was executed under such a cover of urgency, covertness and disinformation:

> *By June 1777, a British takeover of Philadelphia seemed inevitable and imminent. British forces had taken other cities on the eastern seaboard, and it was known that when they took a city, the first thing they did was melt the city's bells in an effort to stalwart communication. As the takeover became imminent, the Continental Congress took action and voted that the Pennsylvania State House bell, the bells of Christ Church Philadelphia, and all metal be removed from the city. A precedent for this action had been set less than a year prior to the British marching on Philadelphia; General Washington carried out the order of a local council that the bells of New York City be removed on September 5, 1776. The New York council's order stated, "The fortune of war…to throw the same into the hands of our enemy, and deprive this State…resource for supplying our want of cannon." On June 16, 1777, the Continental Congress cast a vote to remove Philadelphia's bells, including the Pennsylvania State House bell and the bells of Christ Church, Philadelphia. It must be noted that in addition to the bells of Philadelphia being removed, the colonial government also ordered that all metal be removed from the city to include the rain spouting from houses. General Washington's forces suffered a major defeat at the Battle of Brandywine on September 11, 1777, in a successful attempt to hold the British outside of Philadelphia long enough to transport the bells and other metal out of the city limits and away from British hands. Many theories exist as to why the State House bell, the bells of Christ Church in Philadelphia, and the city's metal fixtures were removed.*

One idea is that the British wanted to melt them down for ammunition and armaments. This theory, while simple and seemingly plausible, is not likely. For the largest army in the world at any given time to come to war without enough weapons to the point that they must melt down metal that is already in the invaded land makes little sense. As bells were used so heavily for communication, it's clear the British intended to permanently decimate the communication system of the American colonists. Melting the bells and entirely destroying them was the best way to achieve this end. If communication was the British's reasoning for melting the bells of a city, the question is then begged, "Why remove the rain spouting and other metal from the city?" For the answer, we must return to the quote from the New York City Council, "And deprive this State…resource for supplying our want of cannon." The bells and metal of Philadelphia were removed in the case that the American army needed to melt the bells for armaments. Thankfully, this need never came about, and the Pennsylvania State House bell remained untouched during its stay in Northamptontown. In June 1778, after the British were forced out of Philadelphia, the bell returned to the Pennsylvania State House; however, the State House's tower was in such disrepair that the bell sat in storage until 1785.[128]

In his research, Reverend Knappenberger explains that Northamptontown was the former name of the city that became known as Allentown. Excepting the detail about the Liberty Bell being in storage until 1785, Reverend Knappenberger's narrative is very much in harmony with the most generally accepted account of most scholars, being very plausible and corroborative with other historical sources that describe the exodus of the State House Bell on a caravan, such as those from historians Whipple and Keyser (author's paraphrase of the two sources with inclusion of other bells follows) :

On the twenty-sixth day of September, in 1777, the British Army was in Philadelphia and had occupied the State House as its headquarters—but not before the State House bell was taken down from the steeple on September 18, 1777, and carried away to safety, along with the bells of Christ Church, Old St. Peter's and other bells, if not all, from Philadelphia's steeples, cupolas and towers were loaded onto the wagons of the Continental Army, which was seven hundred wagons strong, and guarded by two hundred soldiers from Virginia and North Carolina. The bells traveled from Philadelphia to Germantown, then from Germantown to Bethlehem and, finally, Allentown, where they were all unloaded and hidden from the British under

Hiding the State House bell and the other Philadelphia steeple bells under the floorboards of Zion's Reformed Church in Allentown, Pennsylvania. *Drawing by author.*

> *the floorboards of the Zion High Reformed Church. Along the way—while passing through Bethlehem—the wagon carrying the Liberty Bell broke down and had to be unloaded. The bells were away from Philadelphia from September 18, 1777, until June 27, 1778—for the better part of a year.*[129]

For additional information to consider, let us examine another account, which was presented by Reverend Louis A. Rangione in his excellent book *The Liberty Bell's Sister*:

> *The Supreme Executive Council of Pennsylvania, issued orders, September 14th, 1777, for the removal of all of the city's bells. Colonel Benjamin Flower, Commissary General of the Military Stores, was put in charge of the project. In all, eleven bells had to be removed—seven in Christ Church, two in St. Peter's Church, and two in the State House. The combined weight of these bells was estimated to be about 12,000 pounds.*[130]

Given that this order, removing all the city's bells, was carried out to the letter by Colonel Flower, it remains noticeable that absent from the aforementioned list of bells are:

- The bell of the Old Swedes Church, which made the journey, according to Gloria Dei Church historian Jeanette Woehr and oral tradition.
- The bell of St. Paul's Church, because a record of it exists, as discussed earlier.
- The bell of the Walnut Street Prison, which was recorded to have a bell and was referenced previously.
- The 1698 courthouse bell (formerly the Old Market Bell) was well documented in the history of Philadelphia.
- Quite possibly the bell(s) of Second Presbyterian Church, as the records indicate the church desired a bell early on and another bell at a later time. Though the record is ambiguous, it remains entirely likely that the church had at least one bell, if not two.
- The bell from the Union and Hand to Hand Fire Companies of Philadelphia, which was gifted to the city and circulated around different locations in the city before being returned to the firemen, although it was also mentioned in connection with St. James Episcopal Church.[131]
- The small bell of William Penn, which he reportedly brought with him on his voyage to the province in 1682 and was said to have been eventually hung by the entrance door of the State House after it was built, preceding the steeple and the State House bell.

There is much we don't know about the story of the bells that were smuggled out of Philadelphia, and yet, the order of the Supreme Executive Council to Colonel Flower stands firm from September 14, 1777—that *all* bells be removed. What is most important to know is that these artifacts were deemed as "high priority" to the cause of the American Revolution and were handled as such. Could they have been perceived as historic and highly significant icons of the Revolution only a little over a year after the reading of the Declaration of Independence? Or were they significant chess pieces in the overall strategy for winning the war? Or perhaps they were a combination of both estimations concerning their value in the conflict. The latter was most likely the case concerning the evacuation of the bells out from Philadelphia to Allentown, saving them not only from the British Army but also for future generations, for those bells are still extant and remain, thanks to the Hand of Providence in this engagement and all the events that led to the founding of our great nation.

14

RETURN TO PHILADELPHIA • THE STATE HOUSE STEEPLE IS TAKEN DOWN

The Bells Are Rehung

After the State House bell and the accompanying bells of Philadelphia were returned to the city in 1778, there appears to be a void in the historical narrative of the State House bell—at least for a time. Some accounts say that the bell was unloaded in the Yard and neglected for a time, along with one or two other bells. There is much that we do not know about the bells during this time; however, we do know that there was great concern and consternation about the steeple, emanating from the 1775 proposal to the provincial government by architect-builder Robert Smith to take down the structure to the level of the eaves of the building proper and rebuild a cupola in its place. Six years would pass before the demolition work was realized—not by Robert Smith, who sadly died in 1777 at the age of fifty-five, but by Thomas Nevell of the Carpenters' Company of Philadelphia.[132] Nevell's name, also spelled as "Nevill," emerges from the records of the Assembly in 1781 as the man who took down the steeple—not replacing it with a cupola, as proposed by Smith, or rebuilding a facsimile of the original again. Without doubt, the financial strain of the war, especially after the British occupation of Philadelphia, was the principal contributing reason for not rebuilding the steeple at this time—and to be certain, there was a feeling that, by this time, in 1781, the steeple had become more dangerous than it had been a few years before. Perhaps, along with the removal of the bell, stripping the steeple of it's waterproofing metals in 1777 only served to accelerate the process of the structure's decay to a new and dangerous level,

The exiled bells return to Philadelphia. The State House bell and the clock bell remained in the State House Yard until 1781. *Drawing by author.*

as previously discussed. In the recorded words of the Assembly from April 2, 1781, this seemed to be the case:

> *Resolved that the Supreme Executive Council be authorized and directed to have such parts of the Steeple and the State House as are constructed of wood and in a decayed and dangerous condition, taken down; and the remainder sufficiently and effectually covered, in such manner as may be necessary for the preservation of said Building.*[133]

The work began sometime after April 4. Nevell, ever the master of his craft, very obviously studied the situation very closely and persevered in the task at hand with his list of recommendations, of which, the following is very telling—in answering three questions about the bell, regarding:

- the existence of the heavy bell frame as a separate artifact.
- the bell's whereabouts after its return to Philadelphia.
- the identification of the portion of the steeple that was suffering from the problem of decay.

The following entry is from Nevell, who wrote to the Supreme Executive Council on April 16, 1781:

> *All that heavi Fraim whereon the bell used to hang, should come down without delay, which might be done without any materials except Takle & fall &c. And would relieve the other parts of that steeple of a very unnecessary and great weight.*[134]

Let us examine what Nevell's recommendation tells us about the three preceding questions surrounding the bell:

- "All that heavi Fraim": This observation most keenly identifies that the State House bell was hung, mounted, if you will, in a massive timber frame and was not hung in framing that was integrated, or a part of the structure of the steeple.
- "whereon the bell used to hang": Very clearly, Nevell speaks in terms of past tense when describing the frame in 1781—without the bell! This is a tremendous clue about what happened to the bell after it was brought back to Philadelphia in 1778 and supports the premise that the bell was not rehung immediately

in the steeple and very likely remained in the State House Yard from 1778 until July 1781.

- "And would relieve the other parts of the steeple of a great and unnecessary weight": This statement very strongly suggests that other parts of the steeple, though still performing, were very much stressed to the elastic limits of their strength—so much so that the removal of any unnecessary weight, such as the "Fraim," was deemed essential, in order to relieve the stressed structural framing members of the steeple below the level of the cupola. Nevell's work of removing the steeple started at the very top in order to reduce the risk of collapse or failure as it was taken down. Also, this statement most certainly indicates that the damaged portion of the steeple was the portion directly resting on the brick tower and supporting the cupola construction where the beloved State House Bell resided. The heavy timber bell frame could not have been installed anywhere else on the structure, and this figures heavily into why the bell was perceived as a liability to the stability of the steeple.

The "Heavy Fraim" (as Thomas Nevell referred to it) of the State House bell now in storage in the tower of Independence Hall. *Photograph by author.*

By July 16, 1781, Nevell and his company of workmen had completed the work. The steeple had been taken down, and a new roof had been constructed over the top of the brick tower after the bell had been lowered and hung in its frame in the uppermost portion of the brick tower. On August 8, Nevell procured a huge mass of white oak to make a new headstock for the bell.[135] The new roof was utilitarian in nature, and although it was not especially aesthetically pleasing, it was practical and functional—for the new republic, that had weathered the storms of war in proving itself a sovereign nation—with hardly any funding to spare. Nevell described the scope of the work performed when taking down the steeple, lowering the bell and covering the brick tower in a bill submitted to Dr. John Coburn:

> *"The heavy fraim whereon the Bell used to hang" was lowered into the brick tower, and the old Liberty Bell was now again suspended from its beam; the three windows of the otherwise close room were fitted with sounding-boards in order to give full effect to its tones, for alarums, rejoicings, etc. The Tower was plainly though effectually covered for the preservation of the building, and was surmounted by a slender spire or point. Immediately in front of the spire on the main roof, a second bell, called the "clock bell...."*[136]
>
> *And sometimes, the clock bell, confounded with the Liberty Bell, was suspended with a slight covering or shed over it, as is seen in Birch's* Familiar Views of the State House. *The bill for this work is also extant and may interest the curious:*
>
> *Mr. Thomas Nevell,*
> *for the State House. 1781,*
> *To John Coburn, Dr.*
>
> *July 16*
> *To sundry hands getting down the Old Steeple, and getting up the new one, getting up the Bell, and fixing of it...£12 00 00*
> *To the two falls and blocks and Crab getting the Old Steeple down and the new up, and the Bell...£8 00 00 £20 00 00 Note.*
>
> *This is the Rigger's bill against Nevell the Carpenter.*[137]

The years following the dismantling of the statehouse steeple, along with the alteration of the brick tower and rehanging of the State House Bell within, were not uneventful for the bell, as it continued to ring for our new

Lowering the State House bell into the brick portion of the State House tower after the wooden steeple was taken down. *Drawing by author.*

The State House, with the clock bell on the roof, behind the tower, in 1799 by W. Birch and Son. *The Library Company of Philadelphia.*

nation's Congress, July 4 celebrations and other notable events during its era of semi-retirement from the brick bell chamber of the tower:

- October 24, 1781: The surrender of General Cornwallis, signifying the end of British domination over the American colonies.
- April 16, 1783: The Treaty of Paris.
- July 13, 1783: Welcoming George Washington to Philadelphia.
- December 26, 1799: Tolled the death of George Washington.
- December 31, 1799: The last day of the eighteenth century.
- July 16, 1804: Was tolled with the news of the death of Alexander Hamilton.
- July 4, 1806: The thirtieth anniversary of the Declaration of Independence.
- July 4, 1826: The fiftieth anniversary of the Declaration of Independence.
- July 24, 1826: Tolled in memory of Thomas Jefferson and John Adams.
- July 21, 1834: Tolled in memory of LaFayette.

Of course, it was rung more times than the instances listed above, but at times, confirming those occasions has proven difficult. On the occasion of welcoming the Marquis de Lafayette to Philadelphia in 1824, later twentieth-century writers asserted that the bell cracked during that event, but the claims were never substantiated, as the bell was not recorded as having been rung that day. Yet, it continued to ring, and it seems that the loss of the wooden portion of the steeple offered a new life to the bell. And though it was not stationed nearly as high above the State House as it once was, the bell became deeply endeared to every American heart.

15

REBUILDING THE STEEPLE • RETIRING THE OLD STATE HOUSE BELL

A New Steeple, a Tower Clock and a Bell

After the State House steeple was taken down, the State House Bell, which eventually became known as the Old State House Bell, was lowered into the brick tower; the bell's life continued in that solid chamber, still being heard effectively, yet no longer holding the place of prominence, in the vertical sense, and most certainly, its ability to be heard over longer distances was, without doubt, not as great as it was before. Also, the metamorphosis of the steeple into a form resembling an American version of a castle-keep was hardly inspiring to anyone it seems. Of course, the war had severely strained the new republic's finances, which meant that not rebuilding the steeple right away was the only choice at the time, so the shortened tower with a capped roof was the only feasible solution for the fledgling United States of America in the early 1780s. It would be practically another half-century before any real improvements to the tower were made.

These improvements began in 1820, when the Philadelphia Common Council passed a resolution that called for an examination of the clock and clock bell in order to determine whether the need existed to repair the instruments or altogether replace them.[138] As the fiftieth anniversary of the signing of the Declaration of Independence approached, the magnification of the physical needs of the State House only increased, particularly with the visit by the Marquis de Lafayette to the city in 1824, resulting in a plan of action to remedy the building's condition:

The 1828 William Strickland–designed steeple of Independence Hall, which remains faithful to Strickland's original design to this day. *Photograph by author.*

Messrs. Francis Gurney Smith and Benjamin Tilghman of Common Council, and Manuel Eyre and John W. Thompson, of the Select Council, were appointed a committee to carry out the resolution offered by the first named : ——— Resolved, by the Select and Common Councils, That a joint committee of two members from each Council be appointed, to have the turret in the rear of the State House surveyed, and, if found adapted to the purpose, to procure a plan and estimate of the cost of carrying it up to a height sufficient to place a clock and bell therein, to be called the "City Clock," from which the time for the whole city can be regulated.

Messrs. William Strickland, Daniel Groves, John O'Neill, and John Struthers, practical architects and builders, were accordingly called upon to survey the building and submit plans and estimates, on 14th February, 1828. They accordingly stated to the Committee, that having examined the square tower, in the rear of the State House, with reference to its strength and capability of supporting a super-structure, they found that the foundation walls were three feet in thickness at the base, and eighteen inches at the top, being carried up with good substantial brick-work, to the height

> *of sixty-nine feet, having regular offsets on the outside at each of the stories. The walls of the upper story are thirty-one feet square, being tied together with girders; and a strong trussed framing of oak and gum timber; that no departure from stability then appeared in any part of the building, except a slight crack in the southern face of the wall, immediately over the arch of the large Venetian window, which must have occurred shortly after the tower was built; that it had been caused by the opening of the window being so great, as to throw the largest portion of the weight of the walls toward the external angles of the tower; they stated their opinion, however, that this circumstance did not at all affect the strength of the building, and that two stories of brick-work, eighteen inches in thickness, and comprising about twenty-eight or thirty feet in height, could be added to the existing walls with perfect safety; and "by a continuation of the framing alluded to, connecting it with strong diagonal girders, attached by iron clamps to the walls of each of these stories, a wooden cupola and spire," they go on to say, "could be firmly and easily constructed."*[139]

It was architect William Strickland's intention to restore the steeple to its original appearance as much as possible so that it would resemble the steeple of the day when the nation was born on July 4, 1776. In order to fully realize the former steeple, with its intrinsic hour strike, proposals were received in response to the joint committee's solicitation for bids. Isaiah Lukens submitted a proposal for making a new clock, and bell founder John Wilbank submitted a proposal for casting a new bell for the cupola, which were included in the construction estimate presented to the committee at that time:

> *Expenses of carrying up the Turret and Cupola...$8,000*
> *Clock...$2,000*
> *Bell, 4,000 lbs. at 45 cts...$1,800*
> *(Allowed for old Bell $400)...$1,400*
> *$11,400 Cost of painting Turret and incidental expenses...$600*
> *Total estimate...$12,000.*[140]

At this time, the Thomas Stretch clock and the Second bell (the hour-strike bell on the roof) were extant and operating at the State House. Compliments on the Stretch clock were lacking, and perhaps it was Common Council member Benjamin Tighlman who said it best:

The 1828 Isaiah Lukens clock. *From Independence National Historic Park.*

> *If there is anything proverbial, it is the badness of the clock at the State House. It is an excusing not a regulating clock. It is a clock which affords no rule to go by, but a rule not to go by, for everybody knows it can never go right.*[141]

It was indeed a forgone conclusion that the Stretch clock would not continue servicing the State House in the new Steeple, so the awarding of the contract to make a new clock went to Isaiah Lukens, a well-respected

Building the 1828 steeple; the two-ton bell cast by John Wilbank, Philadelphia bellfounder. *Drawing by author.*

and able Philadelphia clockmaker who indeed made the new clock movement, which struck the hour on the clock bell in the forthcoming steeple. What is curious is that the State House had two sizeable bells, either of which could have performed good service (from the foreseeable future in 1828), and yet, a proposal emerged for yet another bell. And we may ask why. Reflecting back on the origins of both bells, which had come to America some seventy-five years earlier, we must remember that the order for the State House bell from the Whitechapel Foundry had to be recast twice by Pass and Stow, and in the end, they had no satisfactory tone. When the Second bell (which became the Stretch clock bell) arrived, its sound was no better than that of the State House bell. Perhaps this is the reason, or one of the main reasons, there was a desire for yet another bell—from an American bell founder no less.

Reflecting on the joint committee's solicitation of bids and the exchange between Council chairman F.G. Smith and John Wilbank, it seems to be an established fact that Mr. Smith asked Mr. Wilbank to produce a bid, and Wilbank responded:

> *Having been called upon by Mr. F.G. Smith, the Chairman of your County, for a proposal to make a bell for the city of Philadelphia.*
>
> *I now submit the following as my proposal for the same. I will cast a bell of any weight, or nearly so, that the Council's may agree upon, at the rate of 45 cents per pound and I will give four hundred dollars for the bell that the clock now strikes upon.*[142]

Wilbank was awarded the bid to make the new committee-prescribed four-thousand-pound bell for the reconstructed State House steeple, and made what was to be a "first bell," but it was rejected due to its unsatisfactory tone. In follow-up, John Wilbank made a second casting, which was hung in the steeple, and although its sound was still somewhat unsatisfactory, it was accepted. Wilbank never removed the State House clock bell from the roof of the State House, as he originally agreed to do, and he was paid for his work by nature of being contracted to do the work.[143] After the bell was hung in the reconstructed steeple, the two-ton Wilbank casting was often looked upon and referred to as the "new State House bell," and indeed, it was fulfilling the duties of its office well. This allowed the Pass and Stow bell to enjoy emeritus status and remain for future generations as an honored icon of the Declaration of Independence and the American Revolution. This may certainly be interpreted as foresight on the part of the Common Council and an important step in preserving the bell for posterity and future generations. As well, Wilbank's refusal to take the Whitechapel clock bell allowed it to see important service again, along with the Stretch clock elsewhere, as we shall soon see.

During this time, visitors to Philadelphia were always interested to inquire after the "Old Independence Bell," and a number of visitors did get to see it in the tower; it was much loved, and growing in affection by the people of America even more as time went on. The marking of the fiftieth anniversary of the Declaration of Independence, along with the reconstruction of the State House steeple, only magnified and reinforced the deepest appreciation and love for the United States and its founding, including the State House, which became known as Independence Hall, and its "Old Independence Bell," which rang for freedom and liberty on that monumental day of July 8, 1776.

16

ST. THOMAS AFRICAN EPISCOPAL CHURCH AND BETHEL AME CHURCH

Were There Bells?

During the Revolutionary era, there was a dual founding, to use the term created by the distinguished scholar and author Lerone Bennett Jr. in his excellent book, *Before the Mayflower*, as the title to his third chapter, "The Founding of Black America."[144] In our discussion about the *Independence Bells of Philadelphia*, it is highly important to present this important period of American history, and especially for us as the much later descendants of our free republic. The story of Black America's struggle for recognition as equals—and as deserving of the same liberty, freedom and rights—as promised in the Constitution—begins much earlier than the period we are examining here, marked by the founding of the Free Africa Society in Philadelphia in 1787 by the "Black pioneers," of which there were eight during this important hour of history.[145] The eight founders of this society were Cato Freeman, Absalom Jones, Joseph Johnson, Richard Allen, William White, Samuel Boston, Caesar Cranchell and James Potter, and yet, of the eight, two founders emerged as the principal leaders of the society—Richard Allen and Absalom Jones. The courage, bravery and daring of these men—and we must not forget the contributions of others too numerous to mention—had a marked effect on the new republic. They were, in a very real sense, a morning star, for those who would take up the cause for the rights of African Americans through the past centuries and to our present day.

During this period, one event stands out, and according to Bennett, it was the first open protest against racial prejudice manifested by white

Left: Reverend Absalom Jones. *Right*: Reverend Richard Allen. *Drawings by author.*

Americans.[146] At the time, Black parishioners were attending services at St. George's Methodist Church, a white congregation, and had been welcome to do so for some time. However, shortly after the establishment of the Free Africa Society, a number of the Society's members, who were regular worshippers at St. George's Church, were literally removed from the worship service one Lord's Day by Trustee members—very shockingly and very cruelly—during the congregational prayer time, while kneeling in prayer. Most notable of the group was Absalom Jones, who was pulled up from his position of kneeling in prayer by one of the church Trustees, as recounted by Richard Allen.[147] The African American congregants, in response, simply stood up and silently made their way out of the church.[148] Following the silent protest and break with St. George's Methodist Church, both men continued their fight for the rights of Black Americans; Absalom Jones led many Black Americans into the Episcopal Church, while Richard Allen founded the African Methodist Episcopal (A.M.E.) Church and later became its first bishop. Absalom Jones founded St. Thomas African Episcopal Church in 1794, the same year in which Richard Allen founded Bethel African Methodist Episcopal Church, reportedly only twelve days apart.[149] Bethel, of course, became known as Mother Bethel and Old Bethel A.M.E. Church later on. Both churches appear to have derived their architectural designs from St. George's, which, in turn, is emblematic of the church design/building precedent in Philadelphia set forth by Robert

Drawing of St. George's Methodist Church of Philadelphia by Frank H. Taylor, circa 1921. *The Library Company of Philadelphia.*

Smith, although Bethel's initial frame was a blacksmith's shop, removed and relocated to the intended church building site.[150]

In both St. Thomas Church and Bethel Church, the lack of a cupola, tower or steeple—in the artist's illustrations we have of the two edifices—begs an important question: Did the churches ever procure a bell for themselves, respectively? It is possible that a bell might have been mounted on a pedestal or pole on the blind side of the artist's rendering; ironically, in the illustration of Bethel Church, there does appear to be a "small bell" on the visible side of the building. Still, we don't have definitive documentation, although the image is compelling, and we hope that St. Thomas may have had a bell as well. Historically speaking, Episcopalians built and worshipped in churches without bell towers. Even if we consult nineteenth-century architect Richard Upjohn's pattern book for rural churches, we find that he has examples of

Right: St. Thomas African Episcopal Church in May 1859, as photographed by Richard Frederick DeBourg. *The Library Company of Philadelphia.*

Below: Drawing of Bethel African Methodist Episcopal Church, by Philadelphia artist W. L. Breton, drawn on stone on July 7, 1829. *The Library Company of Philadelphia.*

ecclesiastical designs which may be built without any tower for a bell. The research of this author turned up no evidence from the available sources of a bell being ordered, hung or rung for either congregation. What might be possible would be the use of a smaller bell that could be rung by two men—or an even smaller bell, like the ones used by town criers. Nonetheless, we always have hope that, perhaps in the future, a new discovery may be made to confirm that bells were part of the services of St. Thomas and Bethel. We may also surmise that, for many churches in America—and indeed worldwide—the cost of erecting and maintaining a sanctuary can be so overwhelming for a struggling congregation that the thought of constructing a tower and hanging a bell therein, is practically impossible. This is especially true of many of Philadelphia's early churches, which bore great likenesses to each other in design, form and materials. In all probability, this was the most likely case for a number of early Philadelphia houses of worship during the days and times of the American Revolution and those following—in a new nation, struggling to stand, through much grit and perseverance, with meager resources—very surely, this is the story of St. Thomas, Bethel and many others. Perhaps the story of a bell may yet be revealed in the stories of these two amazing and courageous churches.

And as a final but most significant point, it seems highly plausible that a number of the members of the congregations of St. Thomas, Bethel A.M.E., and other black congregations in Philadelphia were very involved with the raising, hanging, ringing, lowering and transporting of bells during the Revolution, which would naturally mean that they were also highly involved in the very building of Philadelphia from the very beginning. It would be wonderful to see what future scholarly research and contributions are added to confirm this author's theorem! Without doubt, the founding of America—and the building thereof—could not have happened without the involvement and contributions of African Americans—whether slave or free. May their contributions be fully and completely recognized for their honor and posterity in the story of America.

17

THE EPILOGUE OF THE OLD STRETCH CLOCK AND BELL

The Riotous Mob, Beauty from Ashes

In 1796, Father Matthew Carr of the Order of St. Augustine came to Philadelphia from Dublin, Ireland, to minister to a growing population of German and Irish immigrants in the city.[151] One of the earliest records that attests to the founding of St. Augustine's Roman Catholic Church on North Fourth Street is a document dated June 12, 1796, containing a list of donors who contributed funds for a future church building, which was designed by Philadelphia architect Nicholas Fitzmaurice Fagan and completed in 1801.[152] In 1829, the church's cupola/clock tower was carried up, which was designed by none other than William Strickland, the architect of the reconstructed steeple of the State House.[153] A year later, the priest of the church at that time, Reverend Michael Hurley, purchased the old steeple clock and clock bell from the City of Philadelphia for use in the church's new clock tower; however, the congregation reportedly did not support Reverend Hurley in this transaction, prompting the city to retract the cost and allow the church to use the clock and clock bell on the condition that, in the event the church was removed or demolished, the city would receive them again in good order:

> *Clock and bell shall be and remain in the said church and that the said Pastors and his successors shall have the use of said bell for religious and other purposes; that the same shall not be rung for fires; the expense of keeping the same in repair to be borne by the party of the Second Part* [the City] *and no rent shall be charged by the Party of the First Part.*[154]

St. Augustine's Roman Catholic Church of Philadelphia, circa 1833. *Drawing by author.*

This arrangement was an ideal way for the church to obtain a tower clock and bell, especially with its rapidly growing congregation. However, in the 1840s, anti-Catholic sentiment began festering in Philadelphia, primarily due to the increasing numbers of Irish immigrants in the city. These sentiments reached a fever pitch on May 8, 1844, when, after three days of violent tumult, a riotous mob burned St. Augustine's, along with the rectory.[155] After witnessing the tragic event, watching the flames engulf the steeple of St. Augustine's from the rooftop of his house, a Protestant eyewitness to the tragedy, Andrew Miller, penned the following words in a May 24, 1844 letter to the American Republican Association:

> *I thought of that ancient bell whose tones first proclaimed the glad tidings of American Independence! I turned and saw the reddened spire and roof of that sacred Hall of Independence and the whole high vault of heaven blushing in deep crimson at the scene. I turned aside and wept—not for the ediface or its content, for they were but dross, but I wept over our bleeding constitution—at the so soon forgotten admonitions and precepts*

Above: The ruins of St. Augustine's Church after the fire. *The Library Company of Philadelphia.*

Left: The new bell cast by Joseph Bernhard in 1847 from the fragments of the old bell, now the campus bell of Villanova University, residing at the university's Falvey Memorial Library. *From Digital Library, Villanova University.*

> *of our fathers at the introduction of religious intolerance and religious bigotry into our favored land.*[156]

St. Augustine's was rebuilt and now stands as among the finest examples of church architecture in Philadelphia; however, the Lukens striking tower clock was completely lost in the fire, while the former State House clock bell, though felled and severely damaged by the fire, survived in fragments of its former self. These broken pieces were gathered afterward and used in the casting of a much smaller bell by Philadelphia bell foundryman Joseph Bernhard. The recast bell went to St. Thomas of Villanova College (the college a vision of Father Carr, no less) and became the college bell. It later served for a time as a bell for a church in Jamaica, Long Island, before being returned to Villanova University, where it remains today.[157]

18

THE OLD STATE HOUSE BELL FALLS SILENT

Yet Still Speaking—Loudly

In the years following the rebuilding of the steeple, the Old State House Bell remained active, as we learned in our earlier discussions. There were always opportunities for ringing, but the fact remains that the old bell was never a fire bell.[158] The new State House bell, cast by John Wilbank in 1828, was doing the work that the former State House bell performed during its day; however, the Old State House Bell was still very much sought after to ring for special occasions, and it is generally accepted that the old bell began to show indications of a fracture during this period, which ultimately resulted in the bell's tonal quality being negatively affected, making the old bell less-ringable in terms of swing-ringing. It does appear that the bell could still be rung by pulling its clapper or by being struck with a mallet or hammer, but it seems undeniable that it could not have been rung through swing-ringing in its heavy timber frame as it was before. The following is a select—though not exhaustive—list of occasions when the bell did ring, including notations of when the bell began to show signs of cracking:

- May 1829: After the news of the passage of the Roman Catholic Relief Act (UK), which allowed Irish and English Roman Catholics to serve in parliament.
- July 4, 1832: Rung by all young men of the city and county of Philadelphia for "such time as they deem necessary" to celebrate the anniversary of the Declaration of Independence.

- July 2, 1831: The local newspaper published a notice that the old bell would be pealed from morning until noon and should not be mistaken for a fire alarm.
- February 22, 1832: Rung for George Washington's birthday.
- November 14, 1832: Tolled after the death of the last surviving signer of the Declaration of Independence, Charles Carroll.
- July 22, 1834: Tolled for the death of the Marquis de Lafayette.
- July 8, 1835: Believed to have cracked while tolling for Chief Justice John Marshall's funeral. This is the most widely accepted account of the bell's first fracture.
- April 7, 1841: Was believed to have tolled for the death of President William Henry Harrison as he lay in state in Philadelphia.
- February 22, 1843: The old bell cracked further while celebrating George Washington's birthday—to such an extent that the tone was affected for the worse.

The Liberty Bell and its most renowned feature. *Photograph by author.*

The premise that the crack worsened before February 22, 1846, appears to be very ably supported by the following account:

> *On February 12th, 1846, Philadelphia's Select and Commons Councils asked the Mayor to "cause the Independence Bell to be rung" on Washington's birthday. In order to carry out this resolution, William Eckel, Superintendent of the State House, ordered the crack in the bell drilled out which resulted in the present visible bell-crack. The purpose of this repair was to restore the tone of the bell by placing a small open distance between the two fractured sides of the bell, and possibly, to prevent the crack from spreading. The honor of drilling out the crack had been claimed for Henry Stone, who was a bell hanger at 79 South Fifth Street in 1846. Others claim the crack was redrilled in 1876 by Joseph Bernhard, owner of a foundry on North Sixth Street, foundry employee Thomas L. Durrin and/or Philip Krider.*[159]

From the drilling by Stone, a small bell was made at the request of Eckel, who gifted it to the city council committee on city property. The bell was then given to the Historical Society of Pennsylvania. Stone, Durrin and Krider also made other bells, as did Bernhard from his drilling work in 1876.[160]

We can say with the utmost confidence that although we generally know the window of time in which the bell began to develop the crack and it became worse, we still do not know the exact moment when the crack visibly manifested itself. But from all accounts, it seems very apparent that on the occasion of celebrating George Washington's birthday on February 22, 1846, the last sound of a "whole bell" was heard. But by no means was this the end for the beloved bell. For the next thirty years, the honored bell, which was growing in reputation and stature with each passing year, had much ado made over it and how to display it.

An 1846 idea to relocate the bell to the first floor of Independence Hall was actually realized in 1852, when the bell was in fact lowered to the first floor and placed on an ornamented octagonal base embedded with coats of arms and historical references to the Declaration of Independence, including the signers' names. The bell (itself surmounted by a gilt eagle) was framed by festoons and fasces gracing the American flag—the entire display quite reminiscent of a Roman trophy from antiquity.[161] It was felt that displaying the bell this way would allow visitors to see and experience it up close and on a more personal level. In 1870, there were a couple of well-intentioned ideas which absolutely fell flat—the Common Council of Philadelphia

Right: The Liberty Bell displayed on a Roman dais, as illustrated in *Harper's Weekly*, July 10, 1869. *From the Library of Congress Prints and Photographs Online.*

Below: The Liberty Bell in its original heavy timber frame on display in Independence Hall. *From Etting's* An Account of the Old State House in Pennsylvania.

The Liberty Bell, hung from a massive thirteen-link heavy chain in Independence Hall. *The Library Company of Philadelphia.*

wanted to place the bell in the State House Yard so that the mayor of the City of Philadelphia could toll the bell on the Fourth of July. This idea met opposition from the Select Council and was voted down. Another idea was to mend the bell—or better, restore it—in time for the upcoming Centennial celebration so that it might ring on George Washington's birthday and the Fourth of July by filling the bell's crack with a similar metal in order to restore its sound and tone—this idea went nowhere.[162]

However, in 1872, there was a proposal that was realized when personnel from the navy took on the task of lowering the massive bell frame from the steeple to the first floor of Independence Hall so that the bell could be removed from the octagonal "trophy" display and reunited with its frame, and indeed it was; accordingly, after the bell was rehung in its original frame, it was struck thirteen times with its reattached clapper, ringing "loud and clear for the hearers who were present."[163]

The bell would remain there on the main floor "in-situ" for five years, until 1877, when Philadelphia philanthropist Henry Seybert, whom we shall learn more about later, proposed to suspend the Liberty Bell from the main floor ceiling of Independence Hall (under the tower clock) by a massive thirteen-link chain, itself symbolic of the thirteen original colonies. Seybert funded the project himself, at no cost to the government. Initially, the bell's mounting frame was left outside Independence Hall in order to be disposed of, but this was met with incredible public opposition! The frame was then offered to the Historical Society of Pennsylvania, which turned down the gift, citing spatial constraints as the reason it could not be accepted. In the end, the frame was taken and stored in the tower of Independence Hall, where it remains to this day.[164]

19

BECOMING THE LIBERTY BELL

Symbol of the Abolitionist Movement

Dear reader, in order to discover when the State House bell became known as the Liberty Bell, let us revisit the historical account from Joseph L. Longshore and Benjamin Knowles's work, titled *The Centennial Bell*:

> *It was at the insistence of Mr. Norris, that this new bell was made to bear the beautiful motto: "Proclaim Liberty throughout all the land, to all the inhabitants thereof," which proved to be signally prophetic, for in less than a quarter of a century after, at the reading of the Declaration of Independence in the State House Yard, on Monday, July 8th, 1776, at 12 o'clock, to the populace, it proclaimed the glad tidings of the birth of a new nation, free and independent. From this day it received the distinctive title of the "Liberty Bell," at the sound of which, the fires of liberty were kindled, and orators became eloquent. Its glory has been chanted in song, and its praises rehearsed in story until "Liberty Bell" have become household words in every family, and a theme of veneration on freedom's altar everywhere.*[165]

Unfortunately, the source for this account reference is not given, although the story itself seems very plausible and believable. Since the word *liberty* was inscribed on the bell as part of the Biblical verse taken from Leviticus 25:10 ("Proclaim Liberty Throughout All The Land Unto All The Inhabitants Thereof"), it seems very likely that from the beginning of the Revolution, the bell had started to become synonymous with the fledgling beginning of America, breaking out of its shell and desiring to be free from the rule

The Liberty Bell hung in a French Directoire–Early Republic–influenced carved armature in Independence Hall in Independence Hall. *The Library Company of Philadelphia.*

and tyranny of Great Britain. In the coming years, the bell would also be known as "the Independence Bell" and "the Old State House Bell," as we have previously learned in our discussion. For the most part—at least in what is written—the bell was more commonly called "the State House bell," historically speaking, in the olden times of our nation.

However, in the early nineteenth century, the bell became more broadly known across the United States as a symbol of liberty and freedom, and shortly thereafter, two antislavery publications adopted the bell as its symbol. It was first used in 1837 by an abolitionist publication in New York, entitled *Liberty*, which had a cover illustration of the bell with a subtitle "Proclaim

Freedom" below the drawing of the bell.[166] The second publication was from a Boston-based antislavery group known as the *Friends of Freedom*. This publication was the first to use the term *Liberty Bell* in a published work in 1839. Also around this time, another writer, George Kent, penned a work of poetry that was also titled "The Liberty Bell." This poem was printed in the *Liberator*, an antislavery newspaper. In Kent's work, the bell rings for American freedom, and Kent makes known a request that the bell ring in 1839 for the emancipation of Black Americans.[167]

Top: The illustration of the Liberty Bell on the cover of the *Friends of Freedom* publication, whereby the bell got its most famous, enduring and beloved name. *Public domain.*

Bottom: Maria Weston Chapman. *Public domain.*

Even though the bell began gaining national honor and recognition with the terms *liberty* and *independence* nearly twenty years before—and, as some have contended, even from its beginning—it was much more widely known as the Liberty Bell to the nation when it was adopted by the *Liberty* and *Friends of Freedom* publications during the abolitionist movement for defeating slavery in America during this time. These periodicals were tremendous mediums for antislavery poets and writers, such as Maria Weston Chapman and others, to express their thoughts on the evil practice of slavery and why it should be abolished. Most would agree that these serial publications did a lot in raising the profile and awareness of the Liberty Bell itself. Because of this, the bell also became a symbol of the antislavery movement.

Near the mid-nineteenth century, the bell had more than fully attained the status of being a significant artifact from the American Revolution, inspiring observations like those of James Buckingham, who visited Philadelphia in the 1840s and expressed his thoughts and impressions regarding the bell:

> *This bell (Liberty Bell) though no longer used for general purposes, still occupied the place in which it was originally hung, and like the great bell of St. Paul's in London, is used on special occasions like the Declaration of Independence and visits of distinguished visitors such as Lafayette....It will no doubt be preserved as a national treasure.*[168]

It was also around this time that a fictional story about the Liberty Bell was published; George Lippard's "Fourth of July 1776" is a story about the Liberty Bell being rung on July 4, 1776, by the grandfather of a blue-eyed, flaxen-haired young boy, the messenger in the tale, who tells his grandfather when to ring the bell after the very moment the Declaration of Independence is signed. Although the story was fictional, it became "fact" due to the legitimization of the story by J. Benson Lossing, achieving popularity among readers in America. Nonetheless, the story brought the bell more fame, even though it was a fictional literary work—not a scholarly one![169]

The increasing fame of the bell naturally spilled over into commercial enterprise and commemorative products—to the delight of merchants—its likeness being reproduced for many different products and advertisements, which one may still see to this day, as the bell has never been more popular. Still, during the Civil War, though the bell was popular, it had very little presence and came to represent the North rather than the South, as the bell had already become a symbol of abolition for the Union. However, with the coming of the nation's Centennial in 1876, the Liberty Bell's presence loomed large and was the source of much discussion in the years preceding the event, as being very thematic for the coming celebration.

It would be truly heartening and meaningful if all Americans could know the story of how the bell became so well-known and famous as the Liberty Bell—through the writings of abolitionists long ago who adopted the bell as the emblem of their movement as it signified the very heart of the Constitution, "that all men are created equal," as stated in the Preamble. From the pens of abolitionists to nearly two centuries later, the Liberty Bell continues as a very visible and outward sign of the precepts that our nation's founders set forth in the Constitution. May this knowledge only increase the love and respect for our beloved bell and the principles it embodies and symbolizes for all Americans. As it is written on the bell, from the King James Version of the Bible: "Proclaim Liberty throughout all the Land, unto all the Inhabitants thereof. Lev XXV X."

20

THE CENTENNIAL CLOCK AND BELL OF *1876*

Henry Seybert's "Useful" Gift for the Centennial

Around 1870, Philadelphia began buzzing with excitement in anticipation of the coming Centennial, celebrating America's one hundredth birthday and the passage of a century since the signing of the Declaration of Independence—and Philadelphia was going to celebrate in style. Grand plans were made, and no expenses would be spared in any way in order to have an extravaganza like no other. As we learned before, in 1872, the Liberty Bell's timber frame was lowered by Naval personnel from the tower to the first floor of Independence Hall for exhibition. When they rehung the bell and reunited it with its clapper, it was struck by the clapper thirteen times and reportedly rang out with a loud and clear tone.[170] In 1874, an idea was put forward to build a structure to permanently house the Liberty Bell, with discussion and exploration of the idea continuing into the next year. But this proposal failed to gain any interest or support, and the bell remained in residence in Independence Hall.[171]

At the same time, one of Philadelphia's most prominent and philanthropic citizens, Henry Seybert, was musing on the coming anniversary of America's birth and wanted to do something meaningful for this special occasion. Seybert's desire in life—and in his philanthropy—was not so that he would be "talked about" but that he would "be useful."[172] The very honoring, meaningful and "useful thing" that Seybert did was to have a new clock and a new bell cast for Independence Hall—and what magnificent gifts these were and are, even to this day. Naturally, the gift of the bell displaced the 1828 Wilbank bell in the cupola of the steeple, as did the gift of the new tower clock with respect to the Lukens striking tower clock, which had indeed been striking the hour on the Wilbank bell in the cupola since circa 1830 in the absence of the original clock bell. In order to gain insight into the man and his motive, let us consider Seybert's letter to the Philadelphia Select Council of April 5, 1875:

> *Gentlemen: Feeling considerable interest in the approaching Centennial Celebration of the Declaration of American Independence, and under the conviction that it is the duty of our fellow-citizens to contribute whatever lies in their power to make it a great national success, I beg leave respectfully, with that purpose in view, to make you the following offer, with the request that you will enact such ordinances as will enable the same to be carried into effect.*
>
> *I will enter into an obligation, under a forfeiture of the value of $20,000 in United States bonds, to be deposited with the Pennsylvania Company for Insurance on Lives and Granting Annuities, to have manufactured in our country, and at my expense, a large bell made of the usual composition, to weigh 13,000 pounds, which is as heavy as the steeple will safely bear, and present the same in ample time before the Fourth of July, 1876, to the authorities of the City of Philadelphia, to be erected in the belfry of Independence Hall, with the following inscription upon it, viz.:*
>
> *"July the Fourth, 1876."*
>
> *And the arms of the United States of North America, with their motto "E Pluribus Unum," together with the two Scriptural verses: "Glory to God in the highest and on earth, good will toward men," Luke II, 14. "Proclaim liberty throughout all the land unto all the inhabitants thereof," Leviticus XXV, 10. And the following:*
> *"Presented to the City of Philadelphia,*
> *for the Belfry of Independence Hall in the names of*
> *Adam and Maria Sarah Seybert, and Caroline, their daughter*
> *By their son and brother."*
>
> *I will further agree to have manufactured in our own country a first class City clock of superior workmanship, and present the same in connection with the bell, with the same names inscribed upon it.*
>
> *I beg leave to submit the following programme as part of the ceremonies connected with the observance of our Centennial Anniversary. The bell to be rung for the first time on the Fourth of July, 1876, precisely*

at noon, by striking thirteen peals, one for each of the original states. Simultaneously with the first peal the Scriptural motto, Glory to God in the highest &c, to be telegraphed by the President through the Atlantic cables to foreign nations.

The usual ceremonies of prayer and thanksgiving, the reading of the Declaration of American Independence, and the Emancipation Proclamation, and the delivery of the oration to be followed by seventy-six peals of the bell in recognition of the day to be celebrated. Should sufficient funds be collected to warrant the laying of the cornerstone of a Centennial monument for Independence Square, one hundred peals of the bell to be given on that occasion.

At the close of the day, precisely at midnight, one peal to be sounded for each State and Territory in the Union at that time.

Very respectfully
Henry Seybert,
926 Walnut Street
Philadelphia, April 5th, 1875.[173]

As it turns out, the portion of the inscription bearing his family members' names was deleted, yet as put forth in his letter, Seybert made an extremely grand and generous gesture in his proposed gift for the approaching Centennial.

For his grand clock, which became known as the Centennial Clock, Seybert turned to W.E. Harpur, a watch and chronometer maker on Chestnut Street and also a representative of the Seth Thomas Clock Company of Thomaston, Connecticut.[174] Company founder Seth Thomas (1785–1859), however, was not a watch or clockmaker; he was more of an entrepreneur, whose company had purchased the American Clock Company and then the A.S. Hotchkiss Clock Company in 1872.[175] It followed that all of the watch and clockmaking artisans in those companies then went to work under the Seth Thomas name, as this had become the period of the Industrial Age in America, a time when the mass assembly and manufacturing of products had become the order of the day. The Seth Thomas Clock Company then began to rival its competitor, the E. Howard Watch and Clock Company, which was well known for making excellent and reliable tower clocks, especially in post–Civil War America. The E. Howard Watch and Clock Company worked in tandem with major bell founders to make its clocks synchronize with bells for the best tonal and distance quality. The Independence Hall

The 1876 Centennial Tower Clock of Independence Hall, made by Seth Thomas Clock Company of Thomaston, Connecticut. *Photograph by author.*

The plaque of gift/donation by a "citizen"—none other than Henry Seybert. *Photograph by author.*

tower clock was a special request for Seth Thomas, especially in terms of its size, as it did not fit the profile of the standard tower clocks offered in the Seth Thomas catalog. Rather, it appears that the Seybert clock was an amalgamation of two to three standard tower clock designs from the Seth Thomas Company. The enormity of the clock made all the difference in its design, configuration and mechanical output, which most certainly required the clockmakers to thoroughly verify the parts, instrumentation and hour strike synchronization for such a massive bell. A.S. Hotchkiss, whose firm had been bought out by Thomas, was one of the nation's best clockmakers, who even signed his name to his work while working for the Seth Thomas Company, as is the case on the Centennial Clock itself, appearing on the small dial for tuning alongside the name of the Seth Thomas Clock Company of Thomaston, Connecticut. Of course, the Seth Thomas Company, in emulation of its founder, very surely traded heavily on the longstanding Hotchkiss reputation for making excellent watches and clocks.

A comparison of Independence Hall's Centennial Tower Clock with two of the world's most famous clocks follows:

> [The Centennial Clock's original specifications]:
>
> *8-day gravity-escapement striking tower clock, for use with a heavy bell.*
> *9'- 6 1/2" long x 4'-2 1/4" wide x 8'-3" high (clock mechanism).*
> *6000 lbs./3 tons (total weight of clock mechanism).*
> *14'-0" long pendulum rod of 200 lb. + 500 lb. pendulum bob = 700 lb. total weight.*
> *9'-0" clock-dial plates.*
> *750 lb. weights for the gravity-driven movement of the clock.*
> *(2) 1750 lb. weights for the hour-strike movement for the striking the 6.5-ton clock-bell.*[176]

The dimensional size of Independence Hall's tower clock places it as being commensurate in size with another of the world's most famous tower clocks—the Elizabeth Tower Clock of Parliament, popularly known as "Big Ben":

> [Big Ben (Elizabeth Tower Clock of the Houses of Parliament, London, England)]:
>
> *15'-5" long x 4'-5" wide (clock mechanism).*
> *5 tons (clock mechanism weight).*
> *14'-5" long pendulum.*
> *683 lb. pendulum bob.*
> *23'-0" clock dial diameter.*
> *4 quarter-hour bells, 1 hour-bell (Big Ben).*[177]

And Independence Hall is also proportional to the dimensional size of the Spasskaya, or Savior's Tower Clock in the Kremlin in Moscow, made by the Butenop Brothers of Denmark in 1851:

> [Spasskaya (Savior's Tower of the Kremlin, Moscow, Russia)]:
>
> *12 quarter-hour bells, 1 hour-bell.*
> *12'-0" long x 10'-0" wide x 9'-0" high (clock mechanism frame).*
> *70lb. pendulum.*
> *20'-0" clock dial diameter.*[178]

Regarding the stationary clock bell itself—or, if you prefer, hour-strike bell—the fact that Seybert turned to Clinton H. Meneely and George H. Kimberly for his epic scale bell is quite interesting, given that the company was a relative newcomer to the industry of bell founders, although, in another sense, it was not entirely new to the industry. Clinton Hanks Meneely was the son of the renowned Andrew Meneely, who became a titan in bell casting in America and whose firm was responsible for making an impressive number of bells in the United States, beginning in 1826. When Andrew Meneely passed away in 1851, the foundry went to his sons Edwin and George. More than a decade later, their youngest brother, Clinton, desired a place in the family business after returning home from service in the Union army during the Civil War, yet was denied that opportunity. Clinton therefore had no choice but to open his own bell foundry in partnership with his brother-in-law George Kimberly on the opposite side of the Hudson River in Troy, New York, in 1870, eventually becoming as successful as his father and brothers.

Above: The thirteen-ton Centennial Bell, cast by Meneely and Kimberly of Troy, New York, also the gift/donation from a "citizen." *Photograph by author.*

Left: A view of the front of the Centennial Bell, showing its inscriptions—and its mammoth size. *Photograph by author.*

And Clinton H. Meneely knew his business—most important of which was how to make an excellent bell. A number of the bells cast by Meneely and Kimberly were nominal to large-size bells, meaning that they were likely—and typically—twenty-four to forty-eight inches in diameter, with exceptions of course. But an order like Seybert's was no ordinary order, and very likely required either a modification of an existing casting pit or a new casting pit altogether, as Seybert desired a giant for a bell, which meant that all its parts were enlarged proportionally as well, as one can see very plainly in the following specifications:

- Thirteen-thousand-pound bell—one thousand pounds for each of the thirteen original colonies.
- Seven feet in height.
- Twenty-six feet, six inches, in circumference.
- Three-hundred-pound clapper, nickel-plated.
- Two-hundred-pound striking hammer.
- Cast by Meneely and Kimberly Founders, Troy, New York, 1876.

Another unique feature of the Centennial Bell is its metallurgical composition, made up of 78 percent Atlantic Mine/Lake Superior copper and 22 percent tin, which were smelted together with metal from two cannon from the American Revolutionary War (one American cannon and one British cannon) and two cannon from the American Civil War (one Union cannon and one Confederate cannon). One hundred pounds of metal from each respective cannon were melted in the hot, molten mixture all together, symbolic of peace and unity.[179]

Of course, it was very probable and very likely for the steeple to be reinforced structurally in order to receive such a large bell, which was, at the time of its casting, one of the largest bells in America, and indeed, still is today. When the bell was hung in the tower and rung, the reception of its sound, or tonal quality, seemed to be very positive. Even Seybert himself seemed pleased. However, afterward, the *Philadelphia Press* commented in disappointment on the bell's sound and expressed the need for a new clapper so that the bell might be heard more loudly and more clearly. Amazingly, Seybert was then disappointed in the sound and ordered the bell removed from the steeple in September, recast again to a satisfactory tone and rehung in the steeple again.[180] The name given to the new bell was the "Centennial Liberty Bell," so named because the bell was looked on as a type of new Liberty Bell for the 1876 Centennial.

With all of the interest focused on the new clock and bell, interest in the Liberty Bell's involvement in the Centennial had not waned in the least. Around the same time Seybert was making his plans for his gift, the Philadelphia City Council refused to take action to repair or move the Liberty Bell, but citizens continued to push to have the bell repaired in such a manner that it could be rung on July 4, during the Centennial. Yet, despite a common report that the bell was reviewed and treated to allow for ringing, newspaper accounts of the Centennial celebration do not mention the Liberty Bell being intoned, compared to much coverage about the ringing of the Centennial Bell.[181] Interestingly, shortly after the celebration, Seybert proposed that the Liberty Bell be exhibited in a different way, altogether following the Centennial, that the bell be suspended from the ceiling by a chain of thirteen massive links, which indeed, it was—for a season of time—as we learned previously.[182] For this author, having visited Independence Hall, the idea of suspending the "Great Bell," as proposed by Seybert, would have been stupefying to behold, as it was somewhat an exercise in the gymnastics of static forces—and tectonically unstable in appearance—an entire ton of weight hung from over-one-hundred-year-old framing in the story above! It was an engineering textbook diagram come to life, a two-thousand-pound point load exerting downward force on a major beam. Great artisans-carpenters were those who devised and executed this attraction. This is not to say that the bracing and framing of Independence Hall was not sufficient for the task, but rather, it is a question of connections and methods for achieving this effect. And quite remarkable it was, in exhibiting the bell in a unique and different way. We might say that, in a way, this manner of hanging a bell is not so different in principle than the way the Centennial Bell is hung today in the steeple of Independence Hall, as the mammoth bell is very much a concentrated point load of 6.5 tons. In time, it was necessary to reinforce our beloved Independence Hall throughout with steel in the twentieth century, which was done very skillfully. Perhaps if William Strickland were still living and attending to the work involved in the later steel reinforcing work, it could have been a frightening prospect, even for the very confident Strickland. Perhaps not. Nonetheless, these amazing gifts are and always will be magnificent reminders of that monumental day in 1776, when freedom from tyranny rang out for all Americans. Here, for all time, Henry Seybert is indeed greatly acknowledged and appreciated for his wonderful and "most useful" gifts, which greatly demonstrate such a deep and lasting love and appreciation for America.

21

THE WHEREABOUTS OF THE LUKENS CLOCK AND WILBANK BELL AFTER 1876

Philadelphia's Endowment to Germantown

In 1876, with the installation of the new Centennial Clock and Bell, the nearly-fifty-year-old Lukens clock and Wilbank clock bell were removed from the Independence Hall steeple. For a while, they were stored—but not for long—as they awaited a new life of service elsewhere in the vicinity of Philadelphia.[183]

Discussions for erecting a town hall began in the borough of Germantown around 1847, yet it was not until 1854 that one was built. Designed by Philadelphia architect Napolean LeBrun, this building became known as the Old Town Hall and was used as a hospital during the Civil War. After the Centennial, the steeple of this structure was torn down, and a new tower was erected in its place around 1877.[184] It was during this period that the Lukens clock and Wilbank bell were presented as gifts to the Borough of Germantown and installed in the new tower:

> *At 9 o'clock in the morning on October 4th, 1877, the Hundredth Anniversary of the Battle of Germantown was celebrated by one hundred strokes on the Wilbank bell, and at noon, the Lukens clock was started.*[185]

Over the course of the next forty-five years, these historic horological gifts from the City of Philadelphia seemed to keep good time for the citizens of Germantown. However, the same could not be said for the building proper, as it seemed to have become a Town Hall without a solid use as

Left: The Germantown Town Hall. *From* Historic American Buildings Survey.

Right: The clock tower of the Germantown Town Hall, wherein resided the Lukens clock until 2007. The two-ton J. Wilbank bell remains in the tower to this day. *From* Historic American Buildings Survey.

the seat of local government. It saw a number of varied uses over time, as Germantown consolidated with Philadelphia around 1854, the same year in which the hall was built.[186] Around 1920, the building suffered the fate of demolition; however, a new town hall was erected very expediently afterward on the same site where the old hall once stood. This hall was designed and built to fulfil a charge made by Mayor J. Hampton Moore to bring all the city departments together under one roof.[187] The architect of the new town hall was University of Pennsylvania graduate and Ecole de Beaux-Arts–trained architect John Penn Brock Sinkler, the city's architect, who served in that capacity from 1920 to 1924. Sinkler and a cadre of draftsmen designed all the city's buildings and structures during this time, but eventually, Sinkler resigned from his post in order to give Philadelphia architects the opportunity to design. He disagreed with the nature of the position itself, which was a post that directed all design direction for the city from one person, essentially.[188]

Sinkler went to work on the new design in 1922, modeling it on William Strickland's Merchant Exchange Building at Third and Dock Streets in Philadelphia. Although, it was reported that the White House and Georgian architecture were also sources of inspiration for the building proper, there was also some thought that the tower in Washington and the tower on Independence Hall were design influences in Sinkler's vision for the design of the building's clock tower.[189] The construction of the building was completed in 1925, and anon, the Lukens clock and Wilbank bell began their tenures in the cupola of the new Town Hall. In 2007, the clock was removed and restored and has now experienced a homecoming in the museum of Independence Historic National Park, yet the four-thousand-pound bell remains to this day in the tower. The Lukens clock and Wilbank bell are very key actors in the story of the clocks and bells of Independence Hall; the Lukens clock replaced the Revolution-era Stretch clock, and in the same manner, the Wilbank bell brought an "emeritus status" to the Liberty Bell. How wonderful it would be if the Wilbank bell, truly a very special "Independence Bell of Philadelphia," could experience the same return welcome to the museum of Independence National Historic Park as the Lukens clock did in the early part of the twenty-first century. Perhaps this, too, may come to pass—even yet in the near future.

22

THE JOURNEYS OF THE LIBERTY BELL

Criss-Crossing the Continent by Rail

As opposed to a great number of bells that are hung in their belfries and spend a lifetime there—even for hundreds of years in a number of cases—the Liberty Bell has been a sojourner. As we have previously learned, the bell had been "out of the steeple" early on. And yet, if the founding fathers and the Superintendents of the State House were able to look into the future and see where, why and how the bell would be moved, transported and handled to cities and towns all across the continental United States, what would be their reaction? Since this is a hypothetical question, we can only answer hypothetically. In a way, it is an unfair question, because time, technology, culture and the nation have changed so dramatically. Wouldn't it be interesting to observe Benjamin Franklin inspecting a locomotive or Thomas Jefferson musing and pondering on how the United States so greatly expanded and acquired the very lands that Lewis and Clark reported to him about, all the way to the Pacific Ocean—connected by a new form of transportation known as "the railroad?" This new mode of transportation contributed greatly in traveling great distances in a shorter—and safer—amount of time. But it also introduced more anxiety for our nation's beloved bell, which was in great demand to make appearances in towns and cities across America due to the advent of the "Iron Horse." Of course, from the very beginning of the Liberty Bell's travels, which began in 1885 and ended in 1915, there

The Liberty Bell being loaded for the return trip home after the St. Louis Exposition. *From the Library of Congress Prints and Photographs Online.*

was much protest and objection on the part of many to the very idea of the treasured bell being moved even one foot from its place of repose and display in Independence Hall. Demand for the bell to journey to special events, to make stops at cities and towns along the way, was enormous. It was hard for the mayors and councils of Philadelphia to say no to the several thousands of letters that were coming from schoolchildren, expressing their desires for the bell's presence in their city. Yet the will of the Philadelphia mayors and councils prevailed seven times over a thirty-year period in favor of granting permission for the bell to travel. In every city and town along the route to each destination, the bell was wildly received, lauded and made a spectacle over:

- Philadelphia to New Orleans, Louisiana, 1885: The bell's first journey by rail to the World's Industrial and Cotton Centennial Exposition in New Orleans.[190]
- Philadelphia to Chicago, Illinois, 1893: Journeyed to the World's Columbian Exposition in Chicago.[191]
- Philadelphia to Atlanta, Georgia, 1895: Traveled to the Cotton States and International Exposition in Atlanta.[192]

- Philadelphia to Charleston, South Carolina, 1901: Journeyed to the Carolina Inter-State and Indian Exposition in Charleston.[193]
- Philadelphia to Boston, Massachusetts, 1903: For the 128th Anniversary of the Battle of Bunker Hill.[194]
- Philadelphia to St. Louis, Missouri, 1904: For the Louisiana Purchase Exposition.[195]
- Philadelphia to San Francisco, California, 1915: The last journey of the bell by rail for the Panama-Pacific International Exposition.[196]

With each approval to send the bell to a new destination, objections and protests only increased, though the bell was permitted to be displayed a number of times at local and regional events.

Sadly, there were a number of cities that requested the bell's presence and were turned down:

- Pittsburgh, Pennsylvania.[197]
- Nashville, Tennessee.[198]
- Omaha, Nebraska.[199]
- Jamestown, Virginia.[200]
- Syracuse, New York.[201]
- Portland, Oregon.[202]

The events surrounding the travels of the Liberty Bell are a wonderful tale, and indeed would easily command a number of volumes if they were all thoroughly investigated and recorded for all to read. It is this author's hope that the treatment here of this facet of the bell's history will be taken as the most concise way to disseminate this information due to the limitations of time and space. Nonetheless, the Liberty Bell did, in a great way, reach most of the continental United States, to the delight of the citizenry, making its children joyous, healing old wounds and inspiring a great people.

23

LATER INDEPENDENCE BELLS OF PHILADELPHIA AND AMERICA

Replicated • Patterned after the Liberty Bell

The "canon" of *Independence Bells of Philadelphia* would not be complete without including those later bells that marked an important milestone of social progress, joining in the fight against Communism and celebrating America's Bicentennial. All of these bells were inspired by the beloved Liberty Bell, even if the castings were not exact copies. These bells are worthy subjects of intrigue, investigation and discussion as the "later bells" that echoed the joyous refrain of the Declaration of Independence—liberty—from the historic events of July 8, 1776.

Without doubt, the Liberty Bell is the most celebrated bell in America and among the most celebrated bells worldwide. This fact was reinforced by the Treasury Department in 1950 with the gift of a replica of the Liberty Bell to each state in the Union for their participation in the United States savings bonds program known as the Independence Drive, whereby the Liberty Bell became a symbol of true democracy to strengthen the resolve of the people of the United States against the threat of communism.[203] Each replica bell was cast in bronze by the Paccard Bell Foundry in Annecy, France, to the exact dimensions and proportions of the original Pass and Stow bell, complete with the same inscriptions. The only missing element on each of these bells is the signature crack; they are otherwise compelling replicas to behold.

In residence at the Washington Memorial Chapel at Valley Forge, Pennsylvania, is the Justice Bell, which was originally known as the Women's Liberty and Suffrage Bell for its role in the movement to secure the right

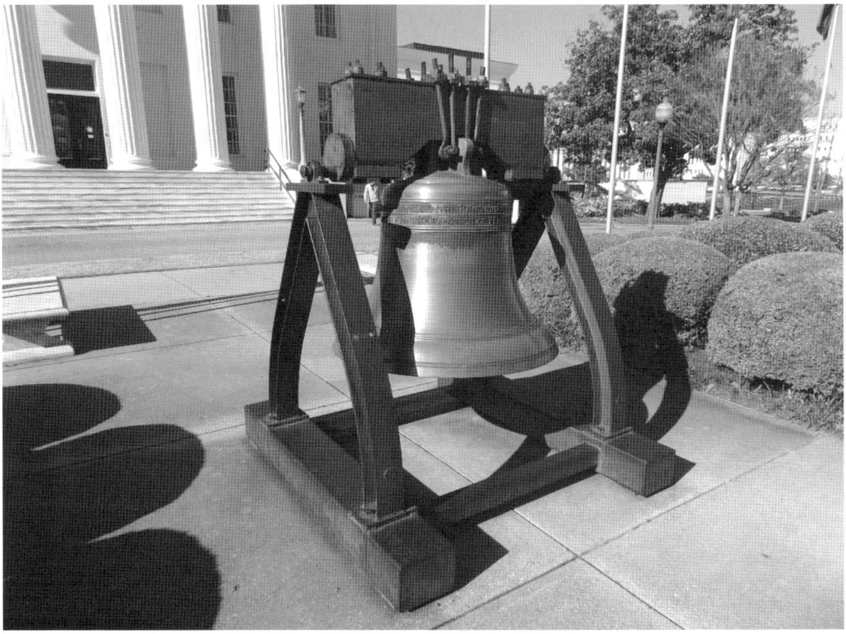

The Independence Drive Liberty Bell replica at the Alabama State Capitol's Avenue of Flags. *Photograph by author.*

The Women's Liberty and Suffrage Bell, now known as the Justice Bell. *Photograph by author.*

for American women to vote in 1919, when the Nineteenth Amendment was passed and ratified. The Justice Bell, conceived as a replica of the Liberty Bell, was commissioned by Katharine Wentworth Ruschenberger (1853–1943), a leader in the Pennsylvania Women's Suffrage Association in Chester County, Pennsylvania, and a member of the National Women's Suffrage Association, the National Women's Suffrage Party and the League of Women Voters. The bell was cast by the Meneely Bell Company of Troy, New York, on March 31, 1915, and weighs one ton (two thousand pounds). The bell bears the following inscription, which is a slight variation from the inscription on the Liberty Bell—taken from Leviticus 25:10, with the heading, "Establish Justice" preceding the biblical quotation and followed by the names of the bellmakers and the date of casting:

ESTABLISH JUSTICE
PROCLAIM LIBERTY THROUGHOUT ALL THE LAND
UNTO ALL THE INHABITANTS THEREOF
MENEELY BELL CO. TROY, NEW YORK MCMXV

During the bell's journeys in the campaign for women's suffrage, the Justice Bell's clapper was chained so that it would not ring, reinforcing the theme that women in America were made silent due to the prohibition against them exercising their constitutional right to vote. Only when victory was won, with the passage and ratification of the Nineteenth Amendment, did the Justice Bell ring on September 25, 1920, in Independence Square in Philadelphia, ringing forty-eight times, once for each state in the Union at that time. The bell was donated to the Washington Memorial Chapel in 1943 at the wishes of Ruschenberger, communicated in her will, and it remains on permanent display today.[204]

During America's Bicentennial in 1976, Great Britain gave America the gift of a bell to commemorate the special occasion. The bell was cast by the Whitechapel Bell Foundry in London, the same foundry that made the Liberty Bell. Queen Elizabeth II and Prince Philip attended the dedication ceremony of the Independence National Historic Park's Visitor Center on Third and Chestnut Streets on July 6, 1976. There, the Bicentennial Bell was installed in the visitor center's 130-foot-tall bell tower a month earlier by a Whitechapel bell hanger. When the Bicentennial Bell was officially presented, the Queen's words were, and are, so meaningful and so timeless for all Americans, Britons, and citizens of all nations, especially today:

The Bicentennial Bell of 1976. *From Independence National Historic Park/National Parks Service.*

On the side of the Bicentennial Bell are the words "Let Freedom Ring." It is a message in which both our people can join, and which I hope will be heard around the world for centuries to come....

To respect the rights of others to govern themselves in their own way.

The Bicentennial Bell is larger than the Liberty Bell, and slightly smaller than the Centennial Bell, as per its following casting information:

Moulds: Begun in January 1976.
Casting Date: March 4th, 1976.
Weight: 12,446 lbs.
Height: 5'-6".
Diameter: 6'-10".
Note: G below middle C.
Composition: Copper and Tin.
Inscription:

"For The
People of the United States of America
From The
People of Great Britain
4 July 1976

LET FREEDOM RING." [205]

All of Philadelphia's and this nation's historic independence bells appear to be in very good condition, and for the most part, have very likely not lost their tone, even today. When bells are cared for and rung properly, they may last centuries. For Philadelphia's and America's Old Independence Bells, this is very possible, and it does appear that these bells are already well on their way to a very good long life of much longevity for the sake of posterity and future generations to come.

24

THE NEXT 250 YEARS

Research and Preservation of Tower Clocks and Bells • Tower Architecture

Given the historic significance of Philadelphia's and America's Bells of the Revolution (and tower clocks as well), with regard to what has been discovered/revealed up to the present, is it ever advisable to cease researching, investigating and exploring to find out more information on our nation's historic bells, or other bells of significance yet to be discovered? Absolutely not! Not only is it necessary, it is crucial to continue scholarly pursuits touching these important artifacts of American history. And so it is for all historically significant American tower clocks and bells, from the dawn of our Republic and leading up to the forthcoming Sestercentennial, our nation's 250th anniversary. What is so amazing is how such discoveries happen—historic records may turn up most anywhere in the form of letters, receipts, records and other forms of documentation. As well, historic tower clocks and bells have also been discovered in the most surprising places in many instances: warehouses, barns, garages and attics, without limitation. It might be astonishing to know how many historic bells there may be in the deep that were shipped directly from the bell foundry to America but never arrived, sinking with their ships and other cargo, slipping away to the bottom of the sea while en route. The same may also be true for vessels that plied the rivers of early America, meeting the same fate. This field of research and study is entirely wide open for investigation and exploration. Let us hope that in the future, those who possess the genuine scholarly interest and passion will lead the way in these pursuits.

Great accolades are due the National Park Service for the excellent work it has done in preserving the Liberty Bell, Bicentennial Bell, and Centennial Bell; would that such veneration and caretaking were so for all of our nation's tower clocks and bells! The author has witnessed many sad cases of tower neglect with regard to historic clocks and bells, even the experience of climbing into a tower, only to find an empty platform with very worn ghosted footprints on the tower floors where the artifacts were once mounted, the emptiness of the space amplified by the sound of the wind whispering its way through the circuits of the sound louvers on all sides. And there are so many stories about these relics that are truly heartbreaking: an old tower clock, made obsolete by a new digital, electronic unit for timekeeping and chiming the hour; the more-than-one-hundred-year-old bell in the tower, propped up by two-by-four-inch wood members on each side to keep the bell from falling over, quite helpless and unable to ring; and then there are the usual structural problems with the steeple or tower itself, weakened in being able to safely support the timepiece and/or bell.

With respect to multiple-bell instruments, such as chimestands or carillons, very real bells have also been replaced by electronic devices that give the impression of a chimestand or carillon, respectively, playing entire sets of songs and/or hymns in carillonneur fashion—and usually from an extremely undersized belfry that might barely contain one or two bells—as if the small aedicule, cupola or steeple is holding a set of fifty bells within it. This begs the question: Does the genuine article and authenticity matter anymore? At present, historic striking tower clocks and tower bells in America are in a state of crisis; they are largely underappreciated, ignored and neglected. The reasons for this present state are numerous and are reflective of civic, social, religious, cultural and technological changes in our country. Because of these contributory elements, the craft itself is beginning to die out, possibly becoming permanently lost. Losing the craft means losing the artisan as well.

For most of the past 250 years in the United States, there have been many tower clockmakers and a plethora of bell foundries due to the great demand for a quickly expanding and developing nation. These clocks and bells were installed in the towers, steeples, domes and cupolas of many American courthouses, schools, colleges, factories, churches and more. Today, the number of American tower clock manufacturers and bell foundries is indeed very slim when compared to the number of these industries in days gone by. Again, the reasons for this are numerous, but one very obvious influence is the effect of a "Beaux-Arts-intolerant"

Modernism on American architecture and technology. Today's modern clock and bell towers are, on the whole, simply not as beautiful as the old ones were. They are more utilitarian-looking due to the discarding of the Beaux-Arts School from architectural education altogether. Today, all architecture must be sustainable, in consideration of the environment and natural resources, which is a noble initiative, and yet, this school of thought prefers the electronic/digital over the foundry-cast article. This is one of the reasons why public tower clocks are disappearing from society. In our cities and neighborhoods, seldom are towers and steeples built to be fitted for traditional timekeeping and striking the hour. In many instances, the vertical elements of architecture are made to simulate the traditional designs in the form of a monolithic shell, purely ornamental in nature and incapable of supporting a tower clock and a bell, necessitating the use of a digital sound system, which may play a repertoire of hymns and melodies intoned by an entire electronic carillon (which exists virtually but is not a real carillon, of course). A real bell may be seen, heard and felt. The experience of hearing electronic chimes, in a number of instances, is similar to hearing a bad record or speaker, and the total experience and impression of sound falls very flat on the hearer. By comparison, hearing real bells is at once very similar to hearing the full effect of a single instrument or an entire orchestra of instruments, which one cannot only hear but feel due to the wonderful polychromatic vibrations.

Let us also examine the case of striking tower clocks, whether they are gravity-driven timepieces, electric motor-driven timepieces or perhaps a combination of the two. Digital timepieces claim absolute perfection to the nanosecond in keeping time, while the archaic tower clock is not as accurate and is more expensive to service and maintain. This claim cannot be disputed, but there is a more important principal involved here: the preservation of history by continuing the great American tradition of the "Town Clock in the Public Square" in towns and cities across our country, since tower clocks and bells are no longer heard on a regular basis, as they once were at the dawn of our nation and well into the mid-latter part of the twentieth century before declining, due to the emergence of the electronic chime system. The author's great concern for the next 250 years and beyond is that these clock towers might become almost completely forgotten due to emerging and future cultural paradigms that favor electronics over those that are made from the earth in a furnace. Electronic devices have their place, but at the same time, the fine arts and crafts of the ages must be preserved and encouraged.

Handmade tower clocks and bells have always been at the very center of hamlets, villages, cities and towns, historically speaking, and define those places in the most unique and site-specific terms, both architecturally and culturally. When one thinks of London, what is the prevailing image that comes to mind? What about Bern? Stockholm? Moscow? English villages? Most county seats in America? College campuses? Philadelphia? It is hoped that this author's point is taken! This tradition of the clock tower as the most outward and visible vertical element in our towns and cities must be preserved, not only with respect to the extant towers, but also in future design endeavors. Architects and builders who execute projects in the language of the classical and traditional must again learn the ancient rules for making beautiful buildings that are appropriate, proportional and contextual, as applicable, and this includes the critical vertical elements of buildings: campaniles, clock towers, domes, steeples and cupolas. Sensitivity must be given to the requirements for the installation of clocks and bells, whether they are striking tower clocks, chimestands or carillons. By continuing this tradition, the retention of *genius loci*, or "spirit of place," of eighteenth-, nineteenth- and twentieth-century America is accomplished in the fullest sense. The use of the traditional clock and bell in everyday American life, installed within the best expressions of traditional and contextual architecture for new construction projects in historic districts, needs to be beautiful as well as functional and optimal for the telling of time and the hearing of bells. The American public should insist on the real—the genuine article in all respects, including architecture, clocks and bells—meaning that the vintage striking tower clocks should be repaired and preserved, and new tower clocks should be reconstructed as new versions of the old. The same practice should apply to bells—repairing the historic ones and continuing to cast new bells in the same tradition as the old bells, hardware and all, mounted on sturdy timber frames. Of course, the digital clock is technologically superior in keeping time, but that is not the point for retaining the historic town clock. They keep reasonably accurate time, but more than this, they keep the idyllic, traditional and beautiful image of the American village, town and city alive, as it was, where citizens may gaze together at the town clock, hear the beautiful tone of the bell and feel the sense of order, security, well-being and beauty that tower clocks and bells contribute to American life, just as they mark this special time of celebration, America's Sestercentennial, our nation's 250th birthday. May it be so, both now and forever!

NOTES

Chapter 1

1. Watson, *Annals*, vol. 1, 10, 35.
2. Ibid., 301.
3. Scharf and Wescott, *History of Philadelphia*, vol. 2, 857.
4. Snyder, *City of Independence*, 28.

Chapter 2

5. Richards, "Old St. Peter's," 162.
6. Ibid.
7. Ibid.

Chapter 3

8. Philadelphia Congregations Early Records, "Second Presbyterian Church (Philadelphia, PA), Congregational, Corporation, and Trustees Minutes, 1749–1775, vol. 1, 17," https://philadelphiacongregations.org.
9. Ibid., 34.
10. Ibid., 46.
11. Peterson, *Robert Smith*, 35.

12. Philadelphia Congregations Early Records, "Second Presbyterian Church (Philadelphia, PA), Congregational, Corporation, and Trustees Minutes, 1749–1775, vol. 1, 112," https://philadelphiacongregations.org.
13. Philadelphia Congregations Early Records, "Second Presbyterian Church (Philadelphia, PA), Congregational, Corporation, and Trustees Minutes, 1792–1803, vol. 3, 54–55," https://philadelphiacongregations.org.
14. Ibid., 57–58.
15. Ibid., 59.
16. Ibid., 60–61.
17. Ibid., 62–64.
18. Ibid., 65.
19. Ibid., 77.

Chapter 4

20. Jeanette Woehr, Gloria Dei Church (Philadelphia, PA), 2020, correspondence.
21. Ibid.
22. Simes, "Sermon," 7.
23. Jeanette Woehr, Gloria Dei Church (Philadelphia, PA), 2020, correspondence.
24. Ibid.
25. Ibid.
26. Ibid., 2, 4.
27. Ibid., 2–3.
28. Ibid., 2.
29. Ibid., 2, 3.
30. Ibid., 2.
31. Ibid., 6.
32. Darrach, *History of the Bell*, 1; Joseph P. Sims, AIA, HABS Survey Report, Gloria Dei Church (Washington, D.C,1937), 3, www.loc.gov.

Chapter 5

33. Barratt, *Outline*, 28; Peterson, *Robert Smith*, 68.
34. Barratt, *Outline*, 41.
35. Peterson, *Robert Smith*, 68.
36. Ibid.

37. Philadelphia Congregations Early Records, "St. Paul's Episcopal Church (Philadelphia, PA), Vestry Minutes, 1762–1774, 13," https://philadelphiacongregations.org.
38. Ibid., 16.
39. Ibid., 79.
40. Ibid., 82.
41. Ibid., 89.
42. Ibid., 92.
43. Ibid., 99.
44. St. Paul's Episcopal Church, Philadelphia, Pennsylvania, (Parish Register, including early Trustee Minutes, 1759–1835) 17," https://philadelphiacongregations.org.
45. Ibid., 22.
46. St. Paul's Episcopal Church, Philadelphia, Pennsylvania, (Vestry Minutes, 1797–1810) 207, 208, https://philadelphiacongregations.org.

Chapter 6

47. Watson, *Annals*, vol. 1, 135–38.
48. Etting, *Historical Account*, 4–7.
49. Ibid., 12; Keyser, *Liberty*, 5, 6.
50. Keyser, *Liberty*, 7; Etting, *Historical Account*, 19.

Chapter 7

51. Etting, *Historical Account*, 26.
52. Peterson, *Robert Smith*, 38.
53. Etting, *Historical Account*, 29.
54. Paige and Kimball, *Liberty Bell of Independence*, 7.
55. Bradshaw, *History and Legends*, 4.
56. Longshore and Knowles, *Centennial Liberty Bell*, 11, 12.
57. Paige and Kimball, *Liberty Bell of Independence*, 7.
58. Bradshaw, *History and Legends*, 5.
59. Ibid.
60. Scharf and Wescott, *History of Philadelphia*, vol. 1, 244–45.
61. Ibid., 245.
62. Etting, *Historical Account*, 31.

63. Ibid.
64. Ibid., 32; Paige and Kimball, *Liberty Bell of Independence*, 11.
65. Etting, *Historical Account*, 32.
66. Eckhardt, *Clocks and Clockmakers*, 86.
67. Etting, *Historical Account*, 32.
68. Ibid.; Paige and Kimball, *Liberty Bell of Independence*, 12.
69. Etting, *Historical Account*, 32; Eckhardt, *Clocks and Clockmakers*, 86.
70. Etting, *Historical Account*, 32.
71. Ibid.

Chapter 8

72. Watson, *Annals*, vol. 1, 378.
73. Ibid.
74. Ibid., 103.
75. Christ Church (Philadelphia, PA), Vestry Minutes, 1717–60, vol. 1, 170.
76. Ibid., 2.
77. Ibid., 26.
78. Ibid., 27.
79. Ibid., 59–60.
80. Ibid., 61.
81. Ibid., 140.
82. Ibid., 144.
83. Accounting Wardens' Steeple Accounts, 1751–1755, 24; Watson, *Annals*, vol. 1, 384.
84. Peterson, *Robert Smith*, 42–43.
85. Adams, "Letter to Samuel Chase."

Chapter 9

86. Nancy Donohue, historian/archivist of Old First United Church of Christ, Philadelphia, April 25, 2022, correspondence.
87. Van Horne, *History of the Reformed Church*, 19–20.
88. Ibid., 23–24.
89. Nancy Donohue, historian/archivist of Old First United Church of Christ, Philadelphia, April 25, 2022, correspondence.
90. Van Horne, *History of the Reformed Church*, 23–24.

91. Nancy Donohue and Dr. Robert A. Schneider, historians/archivists of Old First United Church of Christ, Philadelphia, March 30 and May 2022, correspondence.
92. Nancy Donohue, historian/archivist of Old First United Church of Christ, Philadelphia, April 25, 2022, correspondence.
93. Watson, *Annals*, vol. 1, 451.
94. J.P. Meyer, historian/archivist of Old Zion Lutheran Church, Philadelphia, April 10, 11 and 22, 2022, correspondence.
95. J.P. Meyer, historian/archivist of Old Zion Lutheran Church, Philadelphia, April 25, 2022, correspondence.

Chapter 10

96. Brown, *Carpenters' Company*, vi.
97. Betts, *Carpenters' Hall*, 5.
98. Ibid.; Brown, *Carpenters' Company*, v.
99. Hamlin, *Benjamin Henry Latrobe*, 148–49.
100. Peterson, *Robert Smith*, 115.
101. Betts, *Carpenters' Hall*, 30.
102. Ibid., 35–36.

Chapter 11

103. Peterson, *Robert Smith*, 143.
104. Ibid., 10, 151.
105. Watson, *Annals*, vol. 3, 179–80.
106. Turnbull, *A Visit*, 3.
107. Ibid., 19.
108. Ibid.
109. Ibid., 27–28.

Chapter 12

110. Hoban, *Votes and Proceedings*, vol. 7, 5,941.
111. Hoban, Votes and Proceedings, vol. 8, 6,856.
112. Peterson, *Robert Smith*, 151.

113. Hoban, *Votes and Proceedings*, vol. 8, 7,154.
114. Ibid., 7,220–21.
115. Etting, *Historical Account*, 127–28.
116. Ibid., 82.
117. Keyser, *Liberty*, 13.
118. Hoban, *Votes and Proceedings*, vol. 8, 7,064, 7,157, 7,309.
119. Bradshaw, *History and Legends*, 5.
120. Etting, *Historical Account*, 102–3.
121. Longshore and Knowles, *Centennial Liberty Bell*, 12, 13.
122. Alexander, *Andrew McNair*, 6–7.
123. Adams, "Letter to Samuel Chase."
124. Peterson, *Robert Smith*, 151.

Chapter 13

125. Scharf and Wescott, *History of Philadelphia*, vol. 1, 341–42.
126. Watson, *Annals*, vol. 1, 384.
127. Bradshaw, *History and Legends*, 7–11.
128. Knappenberger, *Liberty Bell at Zion's Reformed*, 3,4.
129. Whipple, *Story of the Liberty Bell*, 118–19; Keyser, *Liberty*, 26–27.
130. Rangione, *Liberty Bell's Sister*, 23.
131. Scharf and Wescott, *History of Philadelphia*, vol. 1, 528.

Chapter 14

132. Paige and Kimball, *Liberty Bell of Independence*, 22.
133. Ibid.
134. Ibid.
135. Ibid.
136. Etting, *Historical Account*, 128.
137. Ibid., 8, 12.

Chapter 15

138. Etting, *Historical Account*, 158–59.
139. Ibid.

140. Ibid., 159.
141. Ibid., 160.
142. Paige and Kimball, *Liberty Bell of Independence*, 25.
143. Ibid., 25–26.

Chapter 16

144. Bennett, *Before*, 55.
145. Ibid., 80; Wesley, *Richard Allen*, 60.
146. Bennett, *Before*, 80–81.
147. Ibid., 81; Wesley, *Richard Allen*, 52–53.
148. Wesley, *Richard Allen*, 53; Bennett, *Before*, 81.
149. Wesley, *Richard Allen*, 78.
150. Ibid., 77–78.

Chapter 17

151. St. Augustine Roman Catholic Church, "225 Years of History."
152. Ibid.
153. Ibid.; Rangione, *Liberty Bell's Sister*, 47.
154. Paige and Kimball, *Liberty Bell of Independence*, 26; Karie Diethorn, chief curator, Independence National Historical Park, National Park Service, U.S. Department of the Interior, May 17, 2022, correspondence; Eckhardt, *Clocks and Clockmakers*, 89.
155. Eckhardt, *Clocks and Clockmakers*, 89–90.
156. Rangione, *Liberty Bell's Sister*, 60–61.
157. Ibid., 65–66.

Chapter 18

158. Paige and Kimball, *Liberty Bell of Independence*, 24.
159. Ibid., 29.
160. Ibid.
161. Ibid., 31–33; Etting, *Historical Account*, 164–65.
162. Paige and Kimball, *Liberty Bell of Independence*, 33.

163. Ibid.
164. Ibid., 35.

Chapter 19

165. Longshore and Knowles, *Centennial Liberty Bell*, 12, 13.
166. Paige and Kimball, *Liberty Bell of Independence*, 80.
167. Ibid.
168. Ibid., 82.
169. Bradshaw, *History and Legends*, 6–7; Paige and Kimball, *Liberty Bell of Independence*, 83.

Chapter 20

170. Paige and Kimball, *Liberty Bell of Independence*, 33.
171. Ibid., 34.
172. Robinson, "Obituary Notice," 255–56.
173. Frazier, "Henry Seybert," 49–50.
174. Ibid., 51.
175. Shelley, *Early American Tower Clocks*, 211–12.
176. Frazier, "Henry Seybert," 51–52; Longshore and Knowles, *Centennial Liberty Bell*, 22.
177. UK Parliament Online, "Great Clock Facts."
178. Galperin, Mark, campanologist and manager, Blagovest Bells (Novato, CA), May 5, 2021, correspondence.
179. Longshore and Knowles, *Centennial Liberty Bell*, 22; Frazier, "Henry Seybert," 53.
180. Longshore and Knowles, *Centennial Liberty Bell*, 22–23; Frazier, "Henry Seybert," 54–55.
181. Paige and Kimball, *Liberty Bell of Independence*, 34.
182. Ibid., 35.

Chapter 21

183. Eckhardt, *Clocks and Clockmakers*, 90; Longshore and Knowles, *Centennial Liberty Bell*, 21.

184. Eckhardt, *Clocks and Clockmakers*, 90; Woodall, *Faded Beauty*.
185. Eckhardt, *Clocks and Clockmakers*, 90.
186. Woodall, *Faded Beauty*.
187. Ibid.
188. Tatman, *John Penn Brock Sinkler*.
189. Clarke, "Sectional City Hall," 534.

Chapter 22

190. Keyser, *Liberty*, 27–28.
191. Ibid., 28.
192. Ibid., 29–31.
193. Paige and Kimball, *Liberty Bell of Independence*, 44.
194. Ibid., 44–45.
195. Ibid., 45–46.
196. Ibid., 49–53.
197. Ibid., 41.
198. Ibid., 43.
199. Ibid.
200. Ibid., 46.
201. Ibid.
202. Ibid.

Chapter 23

203. Paige and Kimball, *Liberty Bell of Independence*, 69.
204. Independence National Historic Park, "Did You Know?"; Justice Bell, "Washington Memorial Chapel."
205. Independence Historical Trust, "Bicentennial Bell Garden"; National Parks Service, "Bicentennial Bell."

BIBLIOGRAPHY

Adams, John. "Letter to Samuel Chase, July 9, 1776." Founders Online, National Archives. www.founders.archives.gov.

Alexander, Mary D. *Andrew McNair and the Liberty Bell, 1776*. Chicago: University of Chicago Press, 1929.

Barratt, Norris Stanley. *Outline of the History of Old St. Pauls' Church, Philadelphia, Pennsylvania*. Philadelphia: Colonial Society of Pennsylvania, 1917.

Bennett, Lerone, Jr. *Before the* Mayflower. New York: Penguin Books, 1968.

Betts, Richard K. *Carpenters' Hall and Its Historic Memories*. Philadelphia: Carpenters' Company, 1891.

Bradshaw, Wellesley. *History and Legends of the Liberty Bell*. Philadelphia: C.W. Alexander, 1876.

Brown, Henry Armitt. *The Carpenters' Company of the City and County of Philadelphia*. Philadelphia: H.C. Coates, 1887.

Christ Church (Philadelphia, PA). Vestry Minutes, 1717–60, vol. 1. Accounting Wardens' Steeple Accounts, 1751.

Clarke, J. Sellers. "Philadelphia's Sectional City Hall." *Architectural Record* 52, no. 6 (1922): 534.

Darrach, Henry, Esq. *History of the Bell of the Gloria Dei Church*. Philadelphia: Gloria Dei Church, 1911.

Diethorn, Karie, chief curator, Independence National Historical Park, National Park Service, U.S. Department of the Interior, correspondence.

Donohue, Nancy, historian/archivist of Old First United Church of Christ (Philadelphia, PA), correspondence.

Eckhardt, George H. *Pennsylvania Clocks and Clockmakers*. New York: Devin-Adair Company, 1955.

Etting, Frank M. *An Historical Account of the Old State House of Pennsylvania*. Boston: J.R. Osgood and Company, 1876.

Frazier, Arthur H. "Henry Seybert and the Centennial Clock and Bell at Independence Hall." *Pennsylvania Magazine of History and Biography* 102, no. 1 (January 1978).

Galperin, Mark, campanologist and manager, Blagovest Bells (Novato, CA), correspondence.

Hamlin, Talbot. *Benjamin Henry Latrobe, 1764–1820*. New York: Oxford University Press, 1955.

HathiTrust Digital Library. www.hathitrust.org.

Hoban, Charles Francis, ed. *Votes and Proceedings of the House of Representatives of the Province of Pennsylvania*. Vols. 7 and 8. Washington, D.C.: Bureau of Publications, 1935.

Independence Historical Trust. "Bicentennial Bell Garden." www.inht.org.

Independence National Historic Park. "Did You Know? The Justice Bell and the Fight for Women's Access to the Vote." www.nps.gov/articles/dyk-justice-bell.htm.

Internet Archive. www.archive.org.

Justice Bell. "Washington Memorial Chapel, Valley Forge." Pennsylvania Online. 2021. www.justicebell2020.org.

Keyser, Charles S. *The Liberty Bell: Independence Hall*. Philadelphia: Dunlap Printing Company, 1901.

Knappenberger, Reverend J.D. *The Liberty Bell at Zion's Reformed Church: How the Hiding of a Bell Impacted the World*. Pennsylvania Historical and Museum Commission, 2019.

Longshore, Joseph S., MD., and Benjamin L. Knowles. *The Centennial Liberty Bell*. Philadelphia: Claxton, Remsen and Haffelfinger, 1876.

Meyer, J.P., historian/archivist of Old Zion Lutheran Church (Philadelphia, PA), correspondence.

National Parks Service. "The Bicentennial Bell." https://www.nps.gov/inde/learn/historyculture/bicentennialbell.htm.

Paige, John C., and David C. Kimball. *The Liberty Bell of Independence National Historic Park: A Special History Study*: Denver Service Center/National Parks Service/United States Department of the Interior, 1988.

Peterson, Charles E. *Robert Smith Architect, Builder, Patriot, 1722–1777*. Philadelphia: Athenaeum of Philadelphia, 2000.

Philadelphia Congregations Early Records. "Second Presbyterian Church (Philadelphia, PA), Congregational, Corporation, and Trustees Minutes, 1749–1772, vol. 1; 1792–1803, vols. 1 and 3." https://philadelphiacongregations.org.

———. "St. Paul's Episcopal Church (Philadelphia, PA), Vestry Minutes, 1762–1774, 1759–1835 and 1797–1810." https://philadelphiacongregations.org.

Rangione, Louis A. *The Liberty Bell's Sister*. Philadelphia: Villanova University, 1976.

Richards, Frederick Lee, Jr. "Old St. Peter's Protestant Episcopal Church, Philadelphia: An Architectural History and Inventory." Master's thesis, University of Pennsylvania, 1992.

Robinson, Moncure. "Obituary Notice of Henry Seybert." *Proceedings of the American Philosophical Society* 21, no. 114 (March 1883): 255–56.

Scharf, J. Thomas, and Thompson Wescott. *A History of Philadelphia*. Vols. 1 and 2. Philadelphia: J.B. Lippincott & Co./L.H. Everts & Co., 1884.

Schneider, Dr. Robert A., historian/archivist of Old First United Church of Christ (Philadelphia, PA), correspondence.

Shelley, Frederick. *Early American Tower Clocks: Surviving Tower Clocks from 1726–1870*. Columbia, PA: National Association of Watch and Clock Collectors, 1999.

Simes, Reverend Snyder B. "Sermon from June 19, 1870." In, *170th Anniversary Gloria Dei (Old Swedes) Church, 1700–1870*. Philadelphia: Gloria Dei (Old Swedes) Church, 1870.

Sims, Joseph P., AIA. HABS Survey Report, Gloria Dei Church. Washington, D.C. 1937, 3.

Snyder, Martin P. *City of Independence: Views of Philadelphia Before 1800*. New York: Praeger Publishers, 1975.

St. Augustine Roman Catholic Church. "225 Years of History and Still Counting." www.st-augustinechurch.com/our-parish.

Tatman, Sandra L. *John Penn Brock Sinkler, Architect Biography, 1875–1959*. Philadelphia: Philadelphia Buildings Online, 2021.

Turnbull, Robert J. *A Visit to a Philadelphia Prison*. Dublin: Robert Napper for John Gough, 1798.

UK Parliament Online. "Great Clock Facts." 2021. www.parliament.uk.

Van Horne, Reverend David. *A History of the Reformed Church in Philadelphia*. Philadelphia: Reformed Church Publication Board, 1876.

Watson, John Fanning Watson. *Annals of Philadelphia and Pennsylvania*. Vols. 1 and 3. New York: Baker and Crane, 1844.

Wesley, Charles H. *Richard Allen: Apostle of Freedom*. Washington, D.C.: Associated Publishers, 1935.

Whipple, Wayne. *The Story of the Liberty Bell*. Philadelphia: Henry Altemus Company, 1910.

Woehr, Jeanette. Gloria Dei Church (Philadelphia, PA), 2020, correspondence.

Woodall, Peter. *Faded Beauty*. Philadelphia: Hidden City Online, 2011.

INDEX

B

C

D

E

F

K

L

M

R

S

T

ABOUT THE AUTHOR

Thomas Kaufmann is an author, architectural historian, preservationist and artist who studied architecture at Auburn University and the Institute of Classical Architecture and Art in New York City, where he now serves as a Fellow Emeritus. He and his wife, Ann Marie, and their son, Tommy, live in a 1926 Craftsman bungalow in the historic Capitol Heights neighborhood of Montgomery, Alabama.